Doing Things the Right Way

Dene Traditional Justice
in Lac La Martre, N.W.T.

Doing Things the Right Way

Dene Traditional Justice
in Lac La Martre, N.W.T.

by
Joan Ryan

Research Partners

Lac La Martre Band Council
Dene Cultural Institute
Arctic Institute of North America

Research Team

Marie Adele Rabesca, Researcher
Diane Romie, Researcher
Lawrence Nitsiza, Researcher
Aggie Brockman, Project Director
Joan Ryan, Principal Investigator

University of Calgary Press
Arctic Institute of North America

© 1995 Joan Ryan. All rights reserved

A co-publication of:

University of Calgary Press
2500 University Drive N.W.
Calgary, Alberta, Canada T2N 1N4

The Arctic Institute of North America
2500 University Drive N.W.
Calgary, Alberta, Canada T2N 1N4

Canadian Cataloguing in Publication Data

Ryan, Joan, 1932–
    Doing things the right way

    Includes bibliographical references and index.
    ISBN 1-895176-62-X

    1. Dogrib Indians—Social life and customs. 2. Law, Dogrib.
3. Indians of North America—Northwest Territories—Lac La
Martre. I. Lac La Martre Band Council. II. Dene Cultural
Institute. III. Arctic Institute of North America. IV. Title.
E99.T56R92 1995   971.9'2004972   C95-910340-6

COMMITTED TO THE DEVELOPMENT OF CULTURE AND THE ARTS

Front cover: Fish smokehouse at Lac La Martre. *Back cover:* Lac La Martre, Summer 1992.
Unless otherwise attributed, all photographs in this book are by Joan Ryan.
The map of the Northwest Territories on page xvi is by Marilyn Croot of Sun Mountain Graphics Services.

∞ This book is printed on acid-free paper. Printed and bound in Canada by Jasper Printing Inc.

*This book is dedicated
to the children of Lac La Martre,
many of whom befriended me while I lived there.
May your lives be ones of strength and happiness
and may you come to experience the serenity
of living in a community dedicated to
"doing things the right way."*

Cousins Amanda and Katrina Jeremick'ca, Summer 1991.

Contents

Abbreviations viii
Foreword ix
Acknowledgments xi
Map of the Northwest Territories xvi
Dogrib Overview xvii
Overview xxv
Elders Interviewed xxxii

1 Introduction 1

2 "Doing Things the Right Way: The Way You Were Taught" 23

3 Family Rules: Rules for Living Together 37

4 Living Politically According to the Dene Ways 51

5 Using the Past to Build a Better Future 65

6 Taking Back Control: Three Case Examples 73

7 Conflicts between Dogrib and Non-Dene Justice Systems 89

8 Conclusions and Recommendations 99

   Reflections on Selected Literature 111
   Bibliography 133
   Index 147

Abbreviations

AINA	Arctic Institute of North America
CAC	Community Advisory Committee
CEC	Community Education Council
DCI	Dene Cultural Institute
DJP	Dene Justice Project
GNWT	Government of the Northwest Territories
HBC	Hudson's Bay Company
JP	Justice of the Peace
PAR	Participatory Action Research
PD	Project Director
PI	Principal Investigator
RC	Roman Catholic
RCMP	Royal Canadian Mounted Police
SSHRC	Social Sciences and Humanities Research Council
TAC	Technical Advisory Committee

Foreword

This has been a difficult book to prepare for several reasons: The Dogrib people have high hopes that the implementation of their recommendations will make significant changes in their lives and help them reclaim responsibility for their own administration of Dogrib justice; the Government of the Northwest Territories (GNWT) and Federal Department of Justice have expectations that its recommendations will lead the way to adaptations in their systems which then will allow them to serve aboriginal peoples in better ways; the funding agencies expect scholarly additions to theory and the ethnographic accounts. Only some of these expectations can be met!

Added to the above expectations is my own need to present the findings in a way which meets both scholarly and useful applications, the latter being of great importance to me.

In addition, there are the problems associated with working with translated materials and the inherent risk of misinterpretation by the scribe. This report is based on the written word in translation and oral discussions – mostly in translation. I cannot include all the things left unsaid because the elders felt no need to repeat them to already knowledgeable Dogrib interviewers.

We, the research team, have tried to guard against misinterpretation by having the preliminary findings and the final draft report verified by all Lac La Martre community elders and by those in other Dogrib communities. However, I hold only myself responsible for errors which might have arisen in this writing process.

As well, I hope that the authorial voice is clear. I have tried to indicate the different times when the text reflects the many voices of the research team, the elders, the non-Dene team members, non-Dene community people, non-Dene court people and advisors and my own reflections. This has not always been easy to do, and it should be understood that, unless I use "I," the writing is mine but the ideas, questions, and issues arise from many discussions in the community and outside it, as well as from the many accounts of the elders. I have tried to write in a language that can be read by the average reader.

The overview of the final project report was translated into all NWT official languages; however, only the Dogrib one is included here.

The biases that appear in the report, which are mine, are identified. For example, the nature of the Participatory Action Research (PAR) methodology, to which I am totally committed, assumes from the start that the community controls the research process, its issues and its results. If one remains consistently at the direction of the community, one cannot pursue directions on one's own. The bottom line is that a PAR methodology assumes that the research team supports participants' and the community's mandates, arrived at by consensus, even when those decisions may not be the most effective in the short term.

I have organized the manuscript in the following ways: I have provided a short and very local background, I have described initial community consultations, the process of starting the project, collecting information, analyzing information, creating recommendations, all of which were verified in Dogrib communities with elders and at public meetings.

I hope I have done the elders, the research team, and the many other people of Lac La Martre "justice." I do have hope that there will be some significant changes based on the recommendations made by the people of Lac La Martre which will make life easier for them and better and more just for all Dene peoples.

Joan Ryan
Principal Investigator
1995

Acknowledgments

In any major project there are many people who play important and vital roles. In naming people and agencies below, I hope I have not omitted others.

The Dene people in the Dogrib region have been very supportive and interested in this project since it began. People in the research community itself have been exceptionally helpful and always supportive. The non-Dene research staff have made friends, enjoyed invitations to special events and have been included in many family happenings. The research team members are grateful to the people of Lac La Martre for their interest, support, and friendship.

Members of the Community Advisory Committee (CAC) have given their time and wisdom to make sure the project went well. This was not always easy. In some instances, it meant disciplining relatives and, in three cases, dismissing them. Nevertheless, people acted with integrity and responsibility and always in the best interests of the project. Special thanks go to CAC members Marie Adele Beaverho, Sophie Williah, Johnny Bishop, Alexis Flunkie, and the late Menton Mantla (elders), Albert Nitsiza (hamlet), Joseph Moosenose (hamlet alternate), Richard Charlo (youth), and Georgie Mantla (youth alternate). The research team learned much from them and shared many good hours with them.

As chairman, Chief Isidore Zoe has given considerable time and effort to the project. The Band Council have always supported the project and hosted the Technical Advisory Committee (TAC) on two occasions.

The Hamlet Council helped us out considerably since we used their fax and copier before getting our own. Millie Nitsiza and Ted Nitsiza were also very generous in providing meeting rooms and rides to the airstrip. We appreciated their help.

The Technical Advisory Committee has continuously encouraged us and has helped to keep the project on track. Members have been enthusiastic visitors to the project area and have lent considerable efforts to finding funds for us with which to do the work and to attend special conferences. We thank them extensively and are grateful for the time they spent with us and for their support and influence.

The Dene Meni Co-op has held our petty cash account, provided special meals for our visitors, and been helpful in several ways.

Therese Jeremick'ca has been our fire tender when we have been away, a service which our computers appreciated especially.

Mary Ann and Charlie Jeremick'ca have kept the house in good shape and provided wood. As well, they have given us moral support and friendship, which we have valued.

Doug Murray, past Principal, affectionately known as "Duck" to the children, provided us with quiet interviewing rooms when the project was in full swing. He also allowed us to store copies of tapes and translations in the school, thus relieving our anxieties about their loss in the event of a fire in our house/office.

RCMP Constable Les Dell and his wife Glenda, Nurse-in-Charge (1990–92) provided us with useful community information. Les provided several information sessions for staff on "the law" and the court process. He was also very helpful in defining legal codes for us when court dockets listed charges by code numbers only. While in the community, Les provided an excellent model of policing based on good communication and intervention, which resulted in few charges being laid against individuals.

The Dogrib researchers could not handle all the Dogrib to English translations of interviews in the project time available so we were grateful to be able to have other Dogrib translators help us out. They were: James Wah-shee, Corrine Nitsiza, Mike Nitsiza, Mary Siemens, Frances Zoe, Margaret Mackenzie, Madelaine Chocolate, Johnny Washie, Phillip Rabesca, Lawrence Nitsiza, and Rachel Crapeau.

John B. Zoe was our cultural advisor and was from time to time the interpreter for some meetings we held in Rae-Edzo. We appreciated his help and advice as well as his family's hospitality while we were in his community.

Jean Pochat, OMI gave us his thoughts on changes from the time he arrived in 1955 to the present. We thank him for his time.

The Arctic Institute of North America (AINA) and the Dene Cultural Institute (DCI) provided core funding, financial administration, friendly advice, moral support and many other services throughout the life of the project. DCI staff Ernie Abel and Wilma Schreder ran errands, got supplies on planes, acquired office furniture for us and did innumerable other things, always cheerfully. As joint partners with the Lac La Martre Band Council, the Institutes were always there to help out in both big and small matters. Many thanks to Joanne Barnaby, Executive Director, DCI, and Mike Robinson, Executive Director, AINA; they always had faith in the project and in the importance of the work.

There were many contributions in kind for the project. Tony Clements, from the Arctic College in Fort Smith provided a computer workshop. AINA provided administrative assistance for the proposal, financial services for the Social Sciences and Humanities Research Council (SSHRC) grant, a computer for the Principal Investigator, and general assistance and support. DCI provided administrative support, did payroll, financial services on all grants except SSHRC, travel arrangements, political support, and many errands. The Dogrib Divisional Learning Centre provided Lucy Lafferty for Dogrib literacy instruction. The GNWT, Culture and Communications, provided Ron Cleary for Dogrib literacy instruction and, as well, reviewed initial translations of interviews. GNWT Justice, provided Betty Harnum for an interpretation and translation workshop. The Lac La Martre Band Council provided political support and hosted the TAC meetings in the community with feasts. The Lac La Martre Hamlet Council provided political support, fax, and photocopying services for a time and provided meeting space for the community consultations. The RCMP provided the services of Constable Dell for two workshops on the law and the court process; as well, he and Constable Roy provided information on cases before the courts.

The Honorable Ethel Blondin-Andrews, MP for Western Arctic, always lent her support to the project and created much good will on our behalf. As well, Ethel chaired an all-day workshop in Montreal, hosted by the Canadian Anthropology Society, which was attended by research staff from the Ft. Good Hope Traditional Environmental Knowledge Project, the Gwich'in Language and Cultural Project at Ft. McPherson, and the Dene Traditional Justice Project at Lac La Martre. It was a great success, and it allowed the Dene researchers to realize how important and significant their work is.

Martha Johnson and Jean-Marie Beaulieu provided a home away from home for me whenever I was in Yellowknife. Jean-Marie loaned us his truck for trips to Rae-Edzo and for shopping for supplies and groceries. I appreciated their support and hospitality.

Al Patenaude of GNWT Justice, helped me obtain obscure references on justice issues, and I gratefully acknowledge the articles he copied for me. This saved me considerable library time. As well, he provided extensive editorial comments on the draft that were very useful. Laurie Nock, Grand Prairie Regional College, also provided comments and asked significant questions which helped clarify my writing.

Crown Counsel Greg Francis provided copies of some cases which related to our work. We appreciated his response to our requests.

Don Avison, former Director of the Aboriginal Justice Directorate of Justice Canada, and former Chief Prosecutor in the Northwest Territories, and now Deputy Minister GNWT Justice has been a good friend to the project, a mentor in developing new ideas and directions both for the project and for northern justice. He challenged me to come to grips with some of the more difficult aspects of the findings. The report is the stronger for his constructive challenges. The feedback on the draft from his staff, was also very useful, and I thank them for their time and thoughtfulness.

Rupert Ross, author of *Dancing with a Ghost*, initiated communication with me by phone during the project. As a lawyer who has been involved with aboriginal people for many years, he has sought through his own practice to learn how things might be done with considerably more cultural sensitivity and appropriateness. He seeks to teach others through his writing. His book was very useful to me in formulating some of the ideas that appear here. However, his sixteen-page written commentary on the draft report helped clarify my writing and thinking even more. I am very grateful to him.

The Northern Justice Society, whose Executive Director, Margit Nance, provided me with research space in their Simon Fraser University Centre, assisted me in finding research reports and the grey literature. The Society provided free access to the copier. I thank them for their collaboration.

The GNWT Department of Justice installed the Dene fonts for the computers, enabling staff to put Dogrib interviews into the database and allowing me to include some Dogrib terms in the report. Also the GNWT Justice translators provided Inuktitut and French translations of the overview for the draft report. Corrine Nitsiza edited the draft Dogrib Overview. Many thanks go to Mary Pepper for her arrangements on these matters.

No project of this sort can take place without major funding from various agencies. Major funding was received from the Social Sciences and Humanities Research Council (SSHRC) and the GNWT Department of Justice. Additional funds were received from Employment and Immigration Canada (Dene/Metis Training Group), Justice Canada (Aboriginal Directorate), the GNWT Department of Culture and Communications (CC), the Dogrib Divisional Board of Education (DDBE), the Arctic Institute of North America (AINA), and the Dene Cultural Institute (DCI). We appreciated the financial and moral support of all those agencies and individuals who contributed dollars and in-kind services.

Suzanne Zwarun helped edit the final report so it would be a tighter and more readable document, and Cathy Schissel did the computer reformatting. I thank them both for their services and for burning the midnight oil with me!

Mike Robinson, Executive Director of the Arctic Institute of North America, raised funds for the publication subvention, without which this book would not have been possible to produce. Many thanks to him.

Finally, since I alone am responsible for the book manuscript, I thank the project staff for their wonderful collaboration, dedicated work and many contributions, which made the project succeed so well. I am grateful that I had the opportunity to work with them and for their continuing friendship and gifts of caribou and fish. I value their phone calls. It is their continuing efforts and successes that make this book valuable and interesting. To Dogrib researchers Lawrence Nitsiza, Marie Adele Rabesca, and Diane Romie a big *masi cho!* Aggie Brockman, Project Director, I thank for handling all the project details, accounts, translations, verification trips and the many other chores she dealt with. I also thank her for being a superb roommate and for her cheery energy.

To all others who showed interest and support, I say *masi cho!*

Joan Ryan
Principal Investigator
1995

The Northwest Territories

ARCTIC OCEAN

ALASKA

YUKON TERRITORY

BRITISH COLUMBIA

GWICH'IN SETTLEMENT AREA

INUVIALUIT SETTLEMENT REGION

ALBERTA

BANKS I.

VICTORIA ISLAND

Rae Lakes •

• Snare Lakes

Edzo • Rae
• Yellowknife (and Ndilo)
• Detah

SASKATCHEWAN

NORTHWEST TERRITORIES

NUNAVUT SETTLEMENT AREA

DEVON I.

ELLESMERE ISLAND

MANITOBA

ARCTIC CIRCLE

HUDSON BAY

BAFFIN ISLAND

GREENLAND

QUEBEC

0
200
400 km

MARILYN CROOT

Dogrib Overview

Dene Cultural Institute, Arctic Institute eyits'ǫ Whatì Kw'ahtideè ginįhtł'èkǫ̀ hazhǫ ełets'àgįįdìi t'à dii Dǫsǫǫ̀łį Nàowoò K'ę̀ę̀ Dǫne Sinìyati wenįhtł'è gįįtł'è hǫt'e.

Social Science and Humanities Research Council eyits'ǫ GNWT Department of Justice sǫǫ̀mba de?ǫ̀atłǫ goghàgįįla. Wedę si sǫǫ̀mba t'à gots'àgįįdìi sìi Arctic Institute, Dene Cultural Institute, Canadian Employment and Immigration Canada, Tłįchǫǫ̀ Nèk'e Enįhtł'èkǫ̀ Gogha K'àodèe, GWNT Culture and Communications eyits'ǫ Justice Canada gots'ǫ sǫǫ̀mba giǫzhah. Wedę si edegha eghàlageeda dǫǫ̀ eyits'ǫ dǫ łǫ la xà?a t'à gogha eghàlagįįdà hǫt'e.

Dii enįhtł'è k'e eghàlagįįda gha sìi Godi Xàeta ts'ǫ K'àowo (PI) gòhłį, Enihtł'è Gogha Sìi?į (PD) gòhłį eyits'ǫ dǫ dį gogha eghàlageeda dǫ tai gitł'axǫ dǫ nàke agejà. Dǫne įłe wetł'axǫ la whe?ǫ sìi eyi sǫǫ̀mba t'à goyatiìchìi k'e etaàgihti sìi ts'àgeèhdi hǫt'e.

Dǫ hazhǫ ełets'àgįįdìi t'à dii enihtł'è k'e eghàladà hǫt'e. Kǫ̀ta dǫ enįhtł'è ts'ǫ k'agedèe ne t'à kèhǫǫ̀wo gots'ǫ enįhtł'è nahǫ̀t'e gots'ǫ̀ ededį enįhtł'è k'e eghàlagįįdà hǫt'e. Kǫ̀ta Gogha K'eyageeti k'e Geèhkw'e (CAC) sìi gik'e eghàlaįdà hǫt'e kw'ahtideè gogha daèhchį k'e įdà.

Kǫ̀ta Dǫ Gogha k'eyageeti k'e Geèhkw'e sìi ǫhdah dį gik'eèhkw'e eyits'ǫ Kǫ̀ta ts'ǫ̀ K'àodèe gots'ǫ dǫ įlè goxè wheda eyits'ǫ Cheko Geèhkw'e gha si dǫ įlè wheda, kw'ahtidèe si gota wheda. Dii Kǫ̀ta Dǫ Gogha K'eyageeti k'e Geèhkw'e sìi dǫ gogha eghàlageeda ts'ǫ̀ k'agedè hǫt'e; dàanì dǫne dats'ehke, dàanì etaàts'ehti, eyits'ǫ dàanì yati ts'ehtsį, eyits'ǫ Godi Xàeta ts'ǫ̀ K'àowo enihtł'è etaàgįhti gots'ǫ̀ ayeh?i si gik'e ełets'àgįįdìi t'à ehkw'i whelàa ageh?į; la hani hazhǫ ts'ǫ̀ k'agedè hǫt'e.

Dàanì Enįhtł'è Weghàlada k'e Geèhkw'e (TAC) si hòèłį. Enįhtł'è dàwhaà ts'ǫ̀ wek'e eghàlageeda ha eyits'ǫ ayìiha aget'į sìi eyi zǫ k'e eghàlageeda ha. Dàanì Enįhtł'e Weghàlada k'e Geèhkw'e gįįlį sìi edegha eghàlageeda dǫǫ̀ gots'ǫ dǫ ìchìi, hanì-le įdè dǫsįnìyati nàowoò gha eghàlageeda gots'ǫ dǫ ìchìi hǫt'e. Dene Cultural Institute gots'ǫ k'àowo įłè gogha daèhchį k'e wheda.

Dǫne Sǫǫ̀łi Nàowoò k'èè̀ Dǫsįnìyati gha godi ehłèts'ele kò dii hats'įįwǫ t'à wek'e eghàlats'įįdà hǫt'e. Done sìi:

1 dats'ǫ nezį ełexè nàgedèe gha nàowoò edegha get'į įłè,
2 nàowoò t'à geda sìi edezha ghàgogehtǫ, hanì dǫ ełetł'axǫedè,
3 dàanì dǫne nàowoò k'èagįt'e agogeh?į įłè,
4 dǫne nàowoò k'èagįt'e-le, nàowoò k'egįįzhìi nįdè dàanì gighàladàa įłè.

Dǫne edegha nàowoò gììt'į ts'įįwǫ įłè sìi ehkw'iats'įįwǫ hǫt'e nǫǫ̀. Nàowoò gììt'į įłè sìi diì gogha nàowoò gǫ̀hłį lanì, wet'à dǫne nezį ełexè nàdèe eyits'ǫ wet'à dǫ edehogihdi si gha hòèłį. Nàowoò xà?a t'à agiat'łį sìi łàa enįhtł'è k'e dek'enègįįtł'èe nile. Hanìkò diì nàowoò gǫ̀hłį lanì nàowoò xà?a t'à gįįdà įłè, nàowoò wòhda dats'ǫ ełèht'e weghàladà, wòhda ełèht'e weghàladà-le eyits'ǫ dǫne hoìla hogehtsį sìi įhk'è hoìla nechà-le, ink'è hoìla nechà.

T'asìi hazhǫ nezį wek'èts'edìi nàowoò, dèe nezį wek'èts'edìi tich'aàdi, dèe k'e t'asìi dehshe, įk'ǫ eyits'ǫ dǫ si, hazhǫ nezį wek'èts'edìi sìi dǫne hazhǫ sìi nezį gik'èezhǫ, wet'a?àa deè ne t'à, dǫne, tich'aàdi eyits'ǫ t'asìi gomoò whela sìi ełet'à eda ne t'à.

Ełexè nàts'edèe nàowoò sìi hots'et'į nàowoò weta whe?ǫ hǫt'e, eyits'ǫ ǫhdah, cheko ayìi laà gits'ǫ ha sìi gha nàowoò gehtsį hǫt'e, nàowoò denahk'e wet'a?àa deè chekoa ghàgogehtǫ. Nǫdeè nįdè chekoa ededį t'asìi hazhǫ hogihdiì agede ha ne t'à.

Eyits'ǫ dǫ gogha k'ade gįįlį gha si nàowoò gǫ̀hłį hǫt'e, weghà ame gogha nàowoò gehtsį, dàanì nàowoò gehtsį eyits'ǫ dàht'e nàowoò hòèłį, eyi nàowoò weghà dǫ hazhǫ dàgot'į sìi gogik'èezhǫ hǫt'e.

Dii haàło nàowoò weghǫ gots'įįde sìi enihtł'è Dèe K'e T'asìi Whela Nàowoò Ełèot'į Gįįlį Nàowoò eyits'ǫ Gogha Dèe ts'ǫ̀ K'àowo Gįįlį

Nàowoò k'e dek'eètł'è hǫt'e. Dǫne ginàowoò hazhǫ ełexè whela lanì kò hanì weghǫ gots'įįde.

Dǫne whaèdǫò k'èè eghàlageeda kò ǫhdah gįįlį sìi dǫ hazhǫ ełek'èè agįįwǫ nįdè nàowoò gehtsį, įlè. Gixè eładįį nèhòkw'i nįdè ǫhdah nàowoò ładį gehtsį hanì-le nįdè nàowogòò gehtsį. K'àodèe gįįlį sìi dǫ nàowoò k'èagįįt'e ha gitł'aà whe?ǫ hǫt'e. Kw'ahtidè eyits'ǫ k'aodèe gįįlį sìi dǫ įk'ǫ elį t'à gots'adi ha gįįwǫ nįdè dagehke.

Chekoà negechà-lia et'iì sįlài gighòo laàtłǫ gots'ǫ nàowoò hoghàgogehtǫ eyi deghà wek'èts'eèzò ats'ejà. Chekoà ghàyatigi?àa t'à hoghàgogehtǫ, gidaà t'àsìi hogehtsį t'à hoghàgogehtǫ, eyits'ǫ goxè gogedo si t'à hoghàgogehtǫ. Chekoà įłaà nechà-lia et'iì la nechà-lia eghàlageedaà agogeh?į eyits'ǫ hǫǫno gighoò aget'į nįdè edèot'į xè eghàlageeda ha dìì-le gogįhwhǫ.

Chekoà edèot'į eyits'ǫ ǫhdah si k'èagįįt'e-le xè gots'ǫ̀ nezį nage?a-le nįdè gikwǫ̀ xè?iìdi įlè hǫt'e. Dǫ yatiì ìchi kò xenagedìi łǫ t'à dǫ xè gogįįdo, dǫ įłè hadi goxè godo, "Įxèę to wet'à nagotsłìitła nàgehtsį-le nįdè k'òkw'įą t'à nàgogehkwa, mòht'a k'omoòdǫǫ̀ edza kò to yìi xàgogeh?à," di.

Eyits'ǫ dǫ dagits'įhke kò hagedi, nàowoò dǫzhi gha hołè eyits'ǫ ts'èko gha nàowoò hołè sìi ełèht'e nile gedi, ełèht'e eghàlageeda-le t'à eyits'ǫ ełèht'e k'ehoge?a-le si t'à, eyi hotiì deghà gots'ǫ̀ hageniidì. Dǫzhia dǫne gìhłè ha nįdè gèotį dǫzhì gįįlį sìi goxè ehdzo tsǫ gogeewa. Įhk'è hoghàdegeetǫ k'e geèhkw'e sìi gigha dìi kò dǫzhia wòhda whachǫ dechįni edegha t'asìi gits'àdi ha kagįįwǫ, dàanì git'à eda ha eyits'ǫ dàanì dǫ nàtso gįįlį ha sìi kagįįwǫ. Giàgįą goxè aget'į, bò si edexè k'egele eyits'ǫ tł'ǫhbàa gòkǫǫ si yìi nagete.

Ekò ts'èkoa t'à gixè hogòht'e-le, ts'èko-ǫhdaà gìhłè ha nįdè ts'imàkǫą yìi yeè whachǫ, dǫ nàdèe ts'ǫ̀ gǫwà nàgedè agogeh?į. Edegha tso hagįįwǫ eyits'ǫ edegha ti si hàgetła, įhk'è gighǫ shètį si hagįįwǫ. Ts'èko wòhda xènagedìi dè, whachǫ ?ǫh gogehdèe lanì ginadì, wòhda t'à whachǫ gįįwǫ xè gixè gotseèdi agòht'e įlè, gedi. Ts'èko wòhda t'à "nàts'etsoò" ats'et'į gedi eyits'ǫ įk'ǫ k'èts'eezhǫ ats'et'į gedi. Ekò wòhda t'à gixè t'asagòjà gįįwǫ-le; ǫhdah įłè wèot'į gits'ǫǫ̀ nageède t'à k'ahjǫ įlè xo ts'ǫ̀ whachǫ nàįdè, di. Dǫ nàgedèe ts'ǫ̀ gowàlia lanì zǫ ts'imàkǫą nàgehge įłè, hanì t'à t'ekoa gitsį, gimǫ eyits'ǫ gidè hani gots'àgehwho, hanì įdè t'ekoa gowhachǫǫ̀ gįįwǫ-le xè t'asìi łǫ hoghàgogehtǫ.

Dakwe whaèdǫǫ̀ ełexè nàgįįdèe kò ełèot'į zǫ lanì elexè nàįdè ìlè. Dǫ nàowoò k'èįzhì nįdè dǫ hazhǫǫ̀ gighǫ ìkw'o hǫt'e. De?ǫ nàowoò k'èįzhì-le, łèt'è ets'ee?į lani nįdè dǫ gighaedlò t'à įzahayìageehtè įlè. Dǫ łèt'è dèè?į nįdè įłè dzęę ts'ǫ̀ łèt'è we?eè k'e dexįį?a ageh?į gà dǫ hazhǫǫ̀ gighaedlò.

Dǫ ehdzǫ ts'ǫ eè?į nįdè sį eèh?į gòhdi ha hǫt'e, eyits'ǫ ts'àwò dèè?į nįdè wexèht'e ts'àwò dǫ ghǫye?a ha hǫt'e, hanì-le dè ts'àwò we?ǫanįįhtìi sìi goghǫye?a ha hǫt'e. Eyi haòt'į nàowoò k'egįįzhìi nįdè (k'àowo) elį, dǫzhi ǫhdaà elį sìi goxè sììgoh?į.

Nàowoò nechà nàatǫ nįdè dǫ hazhǫǫ łàa nègidèe gà dǫ nàowoò k'èįzhìi sìi tani nègįhtèe gà dàanì gighàlada ha sìi ghǫ gogede, hanì įdè ełèot'į hazhǫǫ ełexè nàdèe sìi gixè nezįį anagode ha hǫǫwǫ t'à aget'į. Dǫ wegoht'ǫǫ wek'e nàts'ehdlàa, dǫ xoget'įį ełets'ǫǫ xàgeedèe, eyits'ǫ t'ekoa ts'ǫ ekǫ-le eghàladàa sìi nàowoò nechà k'ets'įįzhìi ghaetà hǫt'e.

Dakwe dǫne nàowoò k'èè dǫ sinìyati nįdè dǫ hojìi eghàlaįdà-le ts'edi k'ègeezhǫ-le įlè. Dǫ hojìi hòèhtsį nįdè dǫ hazhǫ gik'èezhǫ hǫt'e. Amèe wets'ǫ hojìi nàhòwo sìi yek'e xàyaehti ha danàageèh?į, eyits'ǫ amèe ayįla sìi, sį ahłà gòehdi ha danàageèh?į; hanì įdè eyi dǫ at'į sìi dàanì gisinìyahti ha sìi wek'èè gighàlada. Dii hanì ełexè eghàlageeda nįdè dǫzhi ǫhdaà eyits'ǫ ts'èko ǫhdaà ełekèagįįwǫ t'à nàowoò gehtsį hot'e amèe wets'ǫ hojìi nàhòwo sìi wegha ehkw'i anagot'įį, eyits'ǫ dò hazhǫ ts'èhwhį ełexè nàgede anagotį.

Eyi dàagǫjà sìi siagįįlà tł'axǫǫ nįdè, hòt'a wetehoòwo ne t'à weghǫ nagogede-le. Dǫne edaxàgeedè ha nįdè nezį ełexè nàgedèe xè ełets'àgedi nįdè zǫ nezį edegeda ha hǫt'e. Nàowoò k'egezhì nįdè dǫ hazhǫ gixè ekǫ-le agot'į, wets'ih?ǫ dǫ hazhǫ ełexè nàgedèe sìi gixè hoejį, lagot'į, eyits'ǫ dǫ įłàgoet'e agįįt'e sìi gixè si hoejį hò?ǫ ha hǫǫwǫ.

Dii enįhtłè wek'e nàowoò tai ghǫ dǫ dats'įhke t'à wegodìi łǫ xàįtłi, eyi sìi dek'eèhtłè, eyits'ǫ dìi Tsǫtìk'eot'įį dàanì chekoà dǫ ghàts'ehtèe nàowoò eyits'ǫ t'asìi nechà ets'ee?į ghǫ nàyaeti sìi edegha gik'e eghàlageeda ha hogeèhdzà sìi dii enįhtłè k'e dek'eèhtłè hǫt'e.

Eyit'à dǫne giwhaèdǫǫ nàowoò k'èè, Tłįchǫǫ gits'ǫek'e gha sìi ayìi dek'enèts'įįtł' èe sìi asįį weghà Dǫne edeghàlageeda ha dìi-le, eyits'ǫ dìi gogha sìi asįį wet'à edegha nàowogòò gehtsį t'à edeghàlageeda nats'ìchi ha dìi-le hǫǫwǫ. Hę?ę ts'edi ha dìi-le eyits'ǫ įlè si ts'edi.

Įnèę dǫ dàanì edeghàlagįįdàa sìi wet'à dìi gogha hoìla sìidle ha dii. Hanìkò dàagiat'į sìi wets'ǫ nàowoò nezį nagįhchìi gà wek'e nàowogòò gèhtsį nįdè dìi-le ha sǫni. Nàowoò įłè, ǫhdah gits'ǫ nezį nats'e?a, eyi nezįį chekoà hoghàgogehtǫ ha dìi-le hǫt'e, hanì įdè ǫhdah t'asìi k'ègeezhǫ sìi chekoà ghàgogehtǫ įłak'aà gigha nezį sìi k'èè. Ekò ǫhdah cheko k'ayagchti xè dǫ ełegihwhǫ-le nįdè cheko gogìikw'ǫ ha nile eyits'ǫ gots'ǫ nezį k'ehoge?a ha nile, gok'èhoge?à-le agede ha. Ełets'ǫ dǫ agįt'e t'à ełets'ǫ nàgets'oò anagejà nįdè ełek'ayats'ehti hani łǫ whìla agode ha.

Wedę nàowoò nezį łǫ ghǫ gots'įide, weghà dii dzęè gogha dǫne ełek'èedìi ha dìi-le, eyi wexè įk'ǫǫ nàowoò, tich'aàdi nàowoò eyits'ǫ dèe nàowoò k'ègedì eyits'ǫ dàanì dǫ edexogihdi eyits'ǫ dàanì dǫ edet'àgeeda, dǫ eɫeghàgeedi, dǫ eɫek'ègedìi eyits'ǫ wet'à dǫ ayìi dǫ agit'e sìi edek'ègeezhǫ.

Kwet'į k'èè Dǫ Sinįyati k'e geèhkw'e eyits'ǫ Royal Commission Gonè gogha Dǫ Sǫǫ̀ɫį gha Eghàlageeda Dǫ Sǫǫ̀ɫį Sinįyati gha geèhkw'e sìi Kwet'į k'èè Dǫ Sinįyati sìi "ɫadįì dǫ ghàlageeda"nįdè denahk'e Dǫ Sǫǫ̀ɫį gigha nezį ha sǫni, eyi goįtɫǫǫ̀ gighǫ xàyagihti. Whaèdǫ ginàowoò xàts'eeta eyits'ǫ wenįhtɫ'è ts'įįtɫ'è sìi hanì weghàladà ha dek'eèhtɫ'è-le, hanìkò dǫ hagįįwǫ nįdè edįì ɫadįì adle ha sìi ɫadįì at'sele ha dìi-le.

Hanìkò Tsǫ̀tik'eot'įì gots'ǫ ǫhdah eyits'ǫ k'àodèe gįįlį sìi yàazea ɫadįì adle ha gįįwǫ-le; ededį edek'èè dǫsinìyati nàowoò k'èè anagede ha gįįwǫ. Dǫ ɫadįì gighàlahoda nįdè dǫ gixè t'asagode-le agot'į, eyits'ǫ gik'e eghàlageeda ha gįįwǫ-le, dǫ nàke xàʔà sìi įɫèè deghà wek'èè hòʔǫ-le t'à. Kwet'įì gitɫ'axǫ dǫne dezǫ nègets'įįwa gà eyi gilaà įt'įì ehɫèht'e gighàlageeda nįdè wet'à ɫadįì agode ha nile, eyits'ǫ wet'à Dǫne nàowoò k'èè ehkw'i k'àhodèe agede ha nile.

Įnèè nàowoò nezį t'à giat'įì sìi įdaà gogha dàanì wet'à ats'et'į ha wegots'įhʔǫ nįdè eyi sìi la nechà hǫt'e. Hanì hòʔǫ nįdè dǫ hazhǫ kǫta gòla gots'ǫ edegha dǫne sǫǫ̀ɫį gha dosinìyati nàowoò gehtsį ha, wet'à dǫne sǫǫ̀ɫį gha nezį dosinìyati ha, eyits'ǫ ededį eyi la ghàlageeda eyits'ǫ dosinìyati gitɫ'aà wheʔǫ ade ha. Dii enįhtɫ'è wek'e eyi hanì hòʔǫ weghǫ got'sįde hǫt'e.

Dii enįhtɫ'è gots'ǫ nàowoò nechà nàke gòhɫį agòjà, eyi nàowoò nechà nàke sìi enįhtɫ'è k'e gǫtɫǫǫ̀ weghǫ gots'įįde hǫt'e.

1. Tsǫ̀tik'eot'įì ededį dǫ k'èts'edìi nàowoò t'à edegha la nagìchi ha gįįwǫ nįdè, ǫhdah gįįlį sìi ededį xaè dakweɫǫǫ̀ edegha ehkw'i geeda ha hǫt'e. Eyi awèts'edi sìi dǫne dats'ǫ hotìi niwò adedle ha awèts'edi, dǫne sìidegeʔį k'e nègidèe ha hǫt'e, wet'à chekoà eyits'ǫ cheko sìidegedle ha eɫegeèhdi ha, eyits'ǫ ts'èeko si gowhachǫ eɫegeèhdi eyits'ǫ dǫzhi si gowhachǫ eɫegeèhdi nįdè nezį ha. Eɫegeèhdi nįts'ǫ̀, chekoà eyits'ǫ ǫhdah xè edexè sìinagogele ha hǫt'e.

Dzę taàt'e jìetì kalats'edèe ts'įįlį, hanì-le įdè įhk'è jìetì t'à tsįedets'eʔa ts'įįlį sìi wet'à edets'ǫ ts'eèhdlį-le lats'įįt'e. Dǫne gixè t'asìi ha ts'ehʔį ha dìi eyits'ǫ̀ wets'ihʔǫ dǫ edezha k'ègedìi ha dìi, hoghàgogehtǫ t'à nezį gogehshe ha dìi. Jìetì k'alats'edè nįdè wets'ihʔǫ ǫhdah eɫekwǫǫyaà aɫegehʔį, dǫzhi ts'èeko kwǫǫyaàgehʔį sìi eyi denahk'e agot'į hǫt'e. Ts'èeko hazhǫǫ̀ gots'ǫ gogide sìi įnèè ɫǫ xo gots'ǫ̀ dǫzhì gok'alagįįdè įlè, gogedi, t'ekoa gįįlį sìi gixè deʔǫ̀atɫǫ hagòjà įlè, gedi.

Whaèdǫǫ̀ gik'èè agòht'e kò t'asìi ghǫ dǫ kwǫǫyaà agogeh'į įlè. Dǫ hagedi, cheko hanì-le įdè ts'èko ehkw'i eghàlageeda-le nįdè t'asagogehʔį, gedi, ts'èeko ededǫǫ̀ gha edilaà ghàlaįdà-le tahko nįdè eyi hani dǫ gits'ihʔǫ dǫ eɫeta nàgedèe si gixè hoìla agode ha sǫni hǫǫwǫ. Dǫne ekǫ-le eghàlageeda sìi nàgogeh?ǫ t'à gisììhdì-le įlè, wet'à dǫ nezį t'asìi ghàlada ha hanì hoghàgogehtǫ ìlè. Ekò dìi nàts'edèe sìi eyi hanì hoghàgogehtǫ sìi whìle agòjà, eyit'à dats'ǫǫ̀ jìetì wets'ih?ǫ̀ dǫ łǫ t'asìi ghǫ-le ełekwǫǫyaà ełegeh?įį agejà. Įnèę t'à ts'èèko wòhda zǫ gits'ǫ̀ ekǫ-le eghàladàa įlè, gèot'į hanì-le įdè gidǫǫ̀ nezį gok'ègedìi įlè t'à. Ekò dii dzęę̀ gogha sìi ǫhdah jìetì gidoò elį sìi edekęę̀ nezį k'ègedì ha dìi.

Eyit'à wek'e nàowoò hòèlį sìi jìetì k'alats'ewo t'à tsįadets'èè?a sìi tàda gok'eįwo lanì ne t'à eyi lanì weghàlats'eda ha, dek'enèts'įį̀'è. Dǫne Sǫǫ̀łį gots'ǫhk'e dǫne k'aàt'i agogeh?į gįįlį sìi goxè eghàlageeda ts'edi. Dǫne ełeot'į gįįlį įlèhkǫ̀ nàgedèe, cheko si xè, dǫzhi si xè, eyits'ǫ ts'èèko si xè gowhachǫ goxè eghàlageeda ha ts'edi, nezį gixè hò?ǫ agode ts'ǫ̀. Dǫ ededį edegha ehkw'i geedàà agejà nįdè hòt'a kǫ̀ta gogha dosįnìyageti ha dìi-le agede ha.

Dii nàowoò wek'èę̀ agòjà nįdè Kwet'į k'èę̀ nàyaeti sìi whìle agode ha lanì, k'ahjǫ ǫhdah hazhǫt'eè jìetì k'alagįiwo sìi ekǫ-le hogèhtsį t'à. Wek'è agode ha nįdè dǫ tadǫ dèhkw'e t'à Tłįchǫǫ̀ Dǫne Sįnìyagehti hǫłè ha, eyi xè, dǫ sììdege?į k'e nègidèe ha, wet'à k'achį nezį gixè hò?ǫ ha, dǫ ełets'ǫ̀ anagede ha, eyits'ǫ įnèę dàanì ełekwǫǫyaà ałegih?įį sìi t'à edexè sììgogele gha, dǫ geejį-le t'à gixè dàgòjà sìi edeghǫ gogede, chekoa gixè hoìla nàhòwo nįdè eyi t'à denahk'e gighǫ gogįde nįdè nezį ha.

2.   Wedę k'achį nàowoò nàke t'à hòèlį sìi kǫ̀ta dǫ hazhǫ ełexè eghàlageeda t'à dàanì ełexè Tłįchǫǫ̀ dǫsinìyati nàowoò k'e eghàlageeda ha sìi, eyi weghǫ gots'įįde. Cheko eyits'ǫ ǫhdah sìi ełets'ǫ̀ anagede ha hǫǫwǫ sìi weghǫ gots'įįde įlè, eyits'ǫ ǫhdah tani geèhkw'e sìi cheko xè eyits'ǫ̀ ts'ǫǫ̀ko gįįlį, eneèko gįįlį si ts'ǫ̀ anagede ha hǫt'e. K'àodèe yàgįįlį sìi dǫ haàtłǫ xà?a gha gogede ha hǫt'e, eyits'ǫ dǫ hoìla hogehtsį nįdè, hoìla nechà, nechà-le, hazhǫ dàanì sììgele sìi gigòh?à ha hǫt'e.

Nàowoò hòèlį iłè k'e eghàlageeda et'ìi, dǫne nàowoò k'èę̀ dǫsinìyati k'e k'ehogiìhdè ha dìi-le; whaà hoògǫ weghǫ nezį hoghàdegeètǫ xè ełexè gogedo nįdè wek'èę̀ hò?ǫ agode ha. Dǫ įłè gota nàdèe-le sìi dii nàowoò gogha ehkw'i ayįla, eyits'ǫ kǫ̀ta goxè enįhtł'è k'e eghàlaeda, eyits'ǫ nàowoò nezį t'à ts'eeda sìi dek'enèyeetł'è ha, eyi wet'à edahxǫ nàowogòò gogih?à ha sǫni wet'à dǫ nezį ełek'èdìi gha. Dii dàanì gighàlada ha gogih?ǫ nįdè eyits'ǫ kǫ̀ta hę?ę gįįwǫ nįdè Tłįchǫǫ̀ gots'ǫ dǫne nàke gixàehta ha, eyi la gitł'aà whe?ǫǫ̀ ade ha t'asanì-le. Eyitł'axǫ dǫne sǫǫ̀łį k'èę̀ dǫsinìyati k'e nègedè ha hogeèhdza ha dìi-le, nàke xo k'ehǫǫwo nįdè k'achį gik'ǫehta ha, asįį dǫ gigha nezį lì.

Tsǫ̀tì, k'e Gamètì k'e, Wekweètì k'e, Behchokǫ̀, Ndilǫ eyits'ǫ T'è?edaà gots'ǫ ǫhdah gixè kǫ̀ta ełets'aadi t'à nàowoò nechà xàts'įhta sìi eyits'ǫ nàowoò hòèlį sìi dagets'įhke t'à ehkw'i dek'eèhtł'è hǫt'e. Kǫ̀ta dǫ xè ełetsaadìi ts'ih?ǫ̀ dihdę dǫ nàdèe sìi godi nàts'įhtsį sìi gigha ehkw'i whela.

Kǫ̀ta dǫ nàdèe hazhǫǫ̀ Tsǫ̀tik'eot'ìį nàowoò hòèlį k'èę eghàlageeda ha sìi goghǫ mahsì gįįwǫ, ededį si eyi nàowoò xèht'eè gikǫ̀ta gha eghàladàa nįdè gįįwǫ.

Godi Xàgeeta dǫǫ̀: Marie Adele Rabesca, Diane Romie, Aggie Brockman gogha k'àowo elį, eyits'ǫ Joan Ryan, godi xàeta gha k'àowo elį.

Kǫ̀ta Gogha K'eyageeti k'e Geèhkw'e: Kw'ahtideè Isidore Zoe, daèchį k'e wheda edį; Ǫhdah gįįlį: Johnny Bishop, Menton Mantla ni, Alexis Flunkie, Marie Adele Beaverho, Sophie Williah, Kǫ̀ta ts'ǫ̀ k'àodèe gha geekw'e: Albert Nitsiza, Joseph Moosenose; Cheko gha geèhkw'e: Richard Charlo, Georgie Mantla.

Enįhtł'è Hołè Gogha K'eyageeti k'e Dèhkw'e: Joanne Barnaby gogha dàehchį k'e wheda, Dene Cultural Institute (Dǫne Nàowoò k'e Dèhkw'e; Kw'ahtideè Isidore Zoe, Wha Tì Kw'ahtideè Genįhtł'èkǫ̀; George Blondin, Denendeh Elders Council (Ǫdah Denendeh k'e Dèhkw'e); George Cleary/Bill Erasmus, Dene Nation; Angie Lantz/Riki Sato, NWT Native Women's Association (Edzanè Dǫne Ts'èko Eghàlageeda); Michael Robinson, Arctic Institute of North America; Geoff Bickert/ Nora Sanders/Janis Cooper, GNWT Justice (Edzanè Dèets'ǫ̀k'àowo Dǫ sinìyati); Robert Halifax, Chief Judge Territorial Court (Dǫsinìyati dǫǫ̀ dakwełǫǫ̀ wheda Edzanè Dǫ Sinìyati gogha); Sam Stevens, GNWT Justice of the Peace Program (Edzanè Dèets'ǫ̀k'àowo Ts'èwhį Hò?ǫ gha Dǫ Sinìyati); John Dillon/Al Patenaude, GNWT Social Services (Edzanè Dèets'ǫ̀k'àowo Nįhtł'è Ehtsį); Sabet Biscaye, GNWT Culture and Communications (Edzanè Nàowoò & Ełets'ǫ̀ Gots'ede); Don Avison/ Carole LaPrairie/Pierre Rousseau, Canada gha Dèets'ǫ̀k'àowo Dǫsinìyati; Dianne Rattray, MacKenzie Court Workers (Dǫsinìyati xè Eghàgeeda).

Translation by Mary Siemens
Rae-Edzo, N.W.T.

Overview

The Dene Traditional Justice Project (DJP) was a joint venture of the Dene Cultural Institute (DCI), the Arctic Institute of North America (AINA) and the Lac La Martre Band Council.

Major funding was received from the Social Science and Humanities Research Council (SSHRC) and the GNWT Department of Justice. Additional funds were received from the Employment and Immigration Canada (Dene/Metis Training Group), Justice Canada (Aboriginal Directorate), the GNWT Department of Culture and Communications, the Dogrib Divisional Board of Education, AINA, and DCI. Many other services were provided in kind and they are noted in the acknowledgments.

The project had a Principal Investigator (PI), a Project Director (PD) and four Dogrib researcher positions; three researchers were eventually replaced by two others. The money for the remaining position was used to pay for external translation of interview tapes.

The methodology used for the project was participatory action research (PAR), which means that the community owns the project and assumes responsibility for it from start to finish. This responsibility was assumed by a Community Advisory Committee (CAC).

The CAC was composed of four elders and one representative each from the Hamlet and the Youth Group; the Chief represented the Band Council and was the chairman of the Committee. The CAC made all decisions about personnel, helped evolve the interview guideline concepts and terminology, and participated in verifying the results of interviews provided by the research team.

A Technical Advisory Committee (TAC) was also formed to ensure the project stayed on track and remained relevant. The TAC included representatives of interested agencies involved in aboriginal justice issues. It was chaired by the Executive Director of DCI.

The research on traditional justice was based on the following assumptions: that the Dene 1) had a system of rules for making sure the society worked in an orderly way at all times; 2) passed down these rules from generation to generation orally; 3) had ways of enforcing the rules, 4) had ways of dealing with individuals who did not follow the rules, or who broke them.

These assumptions proved to be true. The rules had the intent and spirit of Canadian law.[1] The Dene did not codify their rules and they were not written down. However, rules were classified and were rated by seriousness of the breach. They varied from formal to informal and offences ranged from minor to major.

Rules for stewardship, that is maintaining land, animals, plants, spirits and people in balance, were clear and very important. Survival depended on reciprocal relationships among the human, animal and natural worlds.

Rules for living together included marriage rules, economic and social rules and outlined responsibilities of adults and youth. A major concern was about passing the rules down to children who would eventually take over stewardship.

Rules for political organization made it clear who made which decisions, when and how.

For purposes of discussion we have separated the rules into three categories: natural resource rules, family rules, and rules for local government, even though the Dene system is holistic and completely intertwined.

Traditionally, rules were made by the elders who made their decisions by consensus. Rules were changed, or new rules were developed by elders, as situations changed. Leaders had the responsibility to make

---

1 The term "rule" is used in the text in order to avoid confusion with the western system of "laws."

sure that the rules were followed. The chief and head men could ask for the assistance of the medicine people if they needed guidance.

It is clear that rules were taught to children early, that is from about five years of age. These teachings came in several forms: direct advice, observations, and stories. Children assumed responsibilities early for small chores; by age ten they were expected to be working members of the family unit.

Physical punishment was common if children did not obey or respect parents and elders. Stories told during interviews included memories of being hit with a willow stick and being forced out into cold, dark winter mornings to get dry kindling if one had not done it the night before.

It is also clear from the interviews that some rules were different for males and females, which resulted in different expectations and behaviours of each. For example, young boys approaching puberty were taken out on the trap line by male relatives. While there was some harshness in training and some boys went out on the land alone to seek spiritual guidance and power, they were also provided with companionship, food and warm tents.

In contrast, young girls upon reaching puberty were sometimes isolated in menstrual tipis alone and collected their own wood, water and food. This isolation is remembered by some women as "abandonment"; others described their loneliness and discomfort. While some claim the experience made them "strong" and connected them to the spiritual world, others do not feel that it did so, especially the one elder who was left for almost a year on her own. However, in many cases, menstrual tipis were set close to the main camp so grandmothers, mothers and sisters could visit. This reduced the sense of isolation and allowed older women to teach many things to the young women.

People lived in small groups in traditional times. Therefore, any breaking of the rules was known by the whole camp very quickly. Minor breaches, such as stealing bannock, were dealt with by ridicule. In the examples we have, an effective deterrent was to pin a piece of bannock to the person's jacket for a day, during which time everyone laughed at him or her.

If a person stole from a trap, he had to admit to the theft and replace the fur with one of equal or higher value. Such an offence was handled by the chief's headman who was often the camp's leader. He was known as the *k'àowo* and was usually the most senior male in camp.[2]

---

2 The terms *k'àowo* and *yabahti* are used for head man and chief in order to avoid confusion with the elected chief and council after 1921.

More serious crimes required a gathering of the total local group which placed the individual in the middle of the circle and they discussed ways of dealing with the matter so that family and group harmony could be restored. Serious crimes included rape, adultery, abandoning a family, and impregnating a young unmarried woman.

There was no concept in traditional times of "not guilty." People knew who had done what, waited for the victim to complain, waited for the offender to admit guilt and then dealt with the person as appropriate. The circle process required consensus among the adults, both male and female, and it focused on restitution toward the victim as well as reconciliation and the restoration of group harmony. The focus was on what had caused the person to behave in this way, rather than on the misdeed itself.

Once the matter was dealt with, it was over and was not mentioned again. Survival depended on the goodwill and cooperation of families. Breaking the rules created disorder and imbalance, which was seen as dangerous for the group as well as for individuals.

The book provides many more details of the three areas of rules which researchers asked about and also provides some case examples of current attempts by the people of Lac La Martre to take responsibility for a custody case and a major case of theft.

We turn, then, to the question as to whether the information the Lac La Martre research team have documented about Dene traditional rules, with specific reference to the Dogrib people, might provide some directions and new ideas for the Dene people to take back responsibility for their own ways of social control now.[3]

Many of the practices from the past cannot address current problems. However, if the values attached to those practices could be reclaimed and new practices built on them, then it could work. For example, if the value of respect for elders could be taught to young people in effective ways, then the knowledge of elders could inform youthful behaviour in ways which would be acceptable to both. However, if the elders sit in judgment of youth without mutual respect, then youth will not listen nor act appropriately. If intergenerational bonding could be restored, many of the judgments might be unnecessary.

Other values identified, which could provide the basis for contemporary social control, include spiritual beliefs connected with the animal

---

3 The term "take back" is one used by the Dogrib people to indicate that they feel their responsibilities were taken away from them by non-Dene and they now wish to reclaim them. It does not imply that such responsibilities were ever given up voluntarily, or willingly.

world and the land, self-discipline, self-reliance, sharing with others, caring for others, and a sense of group identity.

There has been considerable discussion by people in the non-Dene justice system and by the Royal Commission on Aboriginal Peoples National Round Table on Aboriginal Justice, about "adaptations" that would make the non-Dene system better for aboriginal people. The research, and the book, does not take that approach, although it would not be difficult to see what adaptations could be made, if desired.

However, the view of the Lac La Martre elders and leaders is that they do not wish to adapt; they want to reestablish their own system. Adaptations tend to neutralize energy and motivation because they do not reflect either side's central views. Putting brown faces where white ones used to be, to do things in essentially the same non-Dene ways, does not lead to change, nor does it give legitimacy or authority to the Dene ways of doing things.[4]

The real challenge is to find ways of taking the positives from the past and to make them work for the future. There is some rationale for this because it means all community members could have the opportunity to design a Dene system and make it work; therefore, they will take on that work and responsibility. Such alternatives are explored within the book itself.

There are two major recommendations which emerge from the book and which are discussed at length within it.

1. Since the Lac La Martre people want to take back responsibility for social control, the adults argue that they have to start by taking back personal responsibility for themselves. This means that individuals need to attain a permanent state of sobriety. Following this, a healing process will be required which will allow for children and youth to meet together to heal. There should also be women's groups and men's groups. At some point, children and adults will have to deal with each other about various abuses.

To be an abuser of alcohol, whether daily or occasionally, is to be disconnected from one's self. This also breaks connections to others and results in a failure of adults to protect children and to help them learn and grow. Alcohol abuse also leads to abuse between adults, especially the abuse of women by men. Every woman interviewee reported abuse by men over the years, often experienced when they were young girls.

---

4 For example, having aboriginal people become justices of the peace does not mean the system they use is theirs; on the contrary, it remains a non-Dene court system.

In traditional times, there appear to have been reasons for punishment by physical means. People stated that there was a connection between a youth's or woman's failure to act in the right way, or to fulfill responsibilities to husbands, which endangered the safety of the group. Such acts were punished harshly in order to teach the person how to do things properly. In current times, the teaching rationale is not there and alcohol is often the trigger that unleashes physical violence. In the past, few young women were sexually assaulted because they were protected by their parents and/or husbands. Currently, alcoholic adults provide no such protection for girls and young women.

The recommendation, therefore, is that alcohol abuse be treated like the epidemic it is. Lac La Marte people requested that a team of native healers be invited to come into the community and that they work with families, youth, men, and women until things start to stabilize. Once personal responsibility is reclaimed, then people can take on community responsibilities for justice.

It should be noted that the implementation of this recommendation likely will decrease non-Dene court charges since almost every single adult crime and some youth offences involve the abuse of alcohol.

If people are to be free to disclose hidden assaults, especially those which involve children, a Dogrib "judgment circle" will be needed, along with a healing process to deal with the past abuse. This process should have as its goals, restitution, reconciliation and healing.

2. The second recommendation addresses the issue of pulling the community together in order to reach consensus about what a Dogrib justice system should look like. As noted above, youth and elders need to reconnect; the middle generation needs to connect with both young and old. Leadership needs to be able to negotiate among groups and establish ways of dealing with offences ranging from minor to major.

This process of building a new system could start while the first recommendation is taking effect; it will take time and education and discussion. People felt it might be useful to have an external facilitator to help put this process in place, to build consensus among community members and to identify values that could lead to innovative ways of maintaining local social control. If available, the two Dogrib researchers could be responsible for this work once a process is identified and agreed to by the community. A pilot justice project could then be put in place and should be evaluated at the end of two years.

The major findings and recommendations in the report were verified at meetings with elders and in public community meetings in Lac La Martre, Rae Lakes, Snare Lakes, Rae-Edzo, Ndilǫ and Detah. As a result of these community meetings, the research team is able to say that there is regional consensus on the findings and recommendations. All the other communities wished the Lac La Martre people success in implementing the recommendations and hoped for similar programs in their own communities.

Research Team: Lawrence Nitsiza, researcher; Marie Adele Rabesca, researcher; Diane Romie, researcher; Aggie Brockman, project director; Joan Ryan, principal investigator.

Community Advisory Committee: Chief Isidore Zoe, chairperson; Elders Johnny Bishop, the late Menton Mantla, Alexis Flunkie, Marie Adele Beaverho, Sophie Williah; Hamlet representative Albert Nitsiza/Joseph Moosenose; youth representatives Richard Charlo/Georgie Mantla.

Technical Advisory Committee: Chair: Joanne Barnaby, Dene Cultural Institute; Isidore Zoe, Chief, Lac La Martre Band Council; George Blondin, Denendeh Elders Council; George Cleary/Bill Erasmus, Dene Nation; Angie Lantz/Riki Sato, NWT Native Women's Association; Michael Robinson, Arctic Institute of North America; Geoff Bickert/Nora Sanders/Janis Cooper, GNWT Justice; Robert Halifax, Chief Judge Territorial Court; Sam Stevens, GNWT Justice of the Peace Program; John Dillon/Al Patenaude, GNWT Social Services; Sabet Biscaye, GNWT Culture and Communications; Don Avison/Carole LaPrairie/Pierre Rousseau, Federal Justice; Dianne Rattray, MacKenzie Court Workers.

Elders Interviewed

Name	Age*	Name	Age
Helen Rabesca	93	Marie Adele Beaverho	61
Louis Beaulieu**	85	Alexis Flunkie	60
Elise Beaulieu	85	Benny Pomie	60
Adele Nitsiza	82	Johnny Nitsiza	59
Johnny Bishop	80	Louis Simpson	59
Marie Madeline Nitsiza	78	Phillip Zoe	59
Mary Louise Bishop	77	Elizabeth Zoe Nitsiza	59
Marie Klugie	77	Jimmy Rabesca	58
Bruno Eyakfwo	76	Marie Flunkie	58
Menton Mantla**	74	Annie Simpson	57
Albert Wedawin	71	Joe Champlain	57
Johnny Beaulieu	70	Harry Beaulieu	55
Phillip Nitsiza	66	Rosa Romie	54
Marie Adele Simpson	66	Madeline Champlain	54
Rosalie Zoe Fish	65	Louis Wedawin	53
Celine Eyakfwo	63	Jimmy Nitsiza	53
Elizabeth Mantla	63	Dora Alexie	52
Marie Adele Moosenose	63	Dora Nitsiza	51
Joe Zoe Fish	63	Francis MacKenzie	51
Pierre Beaverho	62		

Source: Lac La Martre Band List. * Ages as of January 1991. ** Deceased.

1

Introduction

General background

The Dene people have lived in the territories they call Denendeh since time immemorial. Within the Dene Nation are included the tribal groups of Dogrib, Chipewyan, South and North Slavey, and the Gwich'in. This book is based on research done with the Dogrib people of Lac La Martre, but the verification process allows us to generalize for the Dogrib region, which includes the communities of Rae Lakes, Snare Lakes, Detah, Ndilǫ, and Rae-Edzo.[1]

Traditionally, the Dogrib people lived out on the land following a seasonal round of activities which maintained them economically, spiritually, socially and politically. The land, its animals, plants and waters provided food, clothing and shelter. The people were organized in small hunting/trapping and fishing camps based on kinship.[2] Their ties to each other, to

---

1 See the map on p. xvi for the location of the Dogrib communities.

2 See Perry (1989) for discussion of matrilineal versus bilateral preferences in both descent and residence, as well as marriage.

the land, and to the spiritual world were strong and reciprocal. The balance among the human, animal, plant, and spiritual worlds allowed for survival and continuity of Dogrib culture. Many of these spiritual, cultural, and political characteristics have persisted through generations and are evident today, albeit occasionally in differing forms.

The traditional justice system ensured that people understood what the rules were and that they were expected to follow them; that is, socialization ensured that the rules were the base for the normative ways of behaving. These rules were based on social, physical, and spiritual realities and were the only means of survival. They were enforced through the authority of the leader and through consensus of the adults in the camps. The rules were passed down through oral traditions, that is, story telling and advice. They were also reinforced by medicine people.

The Dogrib maintained their society through these oral traditions and the passing down of important belief systems and the teaching of "proper" ways of doing things. It is only recently, in the late 1950s, that English became a second language for the Dogrib people. Today, almost all children understand Dogrib, although some do not speak it, and there are still many elders who do not speak or understand English at all. This strong language base has allowed many oral traditions to continue. However, at least two generations of children have been distanced from this traditional learning because of the takeover of educative responsibilities by non-Dene.

All the Dene people are Athapaskan speakers and they constitute a large majority of the population in the Western Arctic, which spans north-south from the Alberta border to the MacKenzie Delta, and east-west from the Yukon border to the Inuit Territories of Nunavut. The Dene populations were traditionally sparse and spread over many miles of land. Times were not always easy and both disease (smallpox, influenza, tuberculosis) and food shortages took their toll over the centuries.[3] The advent of the fur trade encouraged seasonal gatherings and eventually led to more permanent settlement in communities at the trading posts, and nearby. The arrival of missionaries with schools and sometimes hospitals, and the imposition of Canadian government administration of the Dene people and their territories in the late 1940s and 1950s led to further permanent settlement in communities. As well, the 1921 Treaty imposed the Indian Act upon the Dene with the resulting changes in

---

3 Hearne's reports indicate that in the Chipewyan area in the late 1700s, 90% of the population succumbed to smallpox. He attributes the success of the gun-bearing Crees in the fur trade to taking over some of the Chipewyan territories. (Halliday, W.E., *Canada Mines and Resources Bulletin* 89, 1937.)

political organization and the growth of dependency on non-Dene institutions. Unlike other aboriginal groups throughout Canada, the Dene were not wards of the government nor were they assigned reserves.

The contact period, in the late 1700s, brought guns, the fur trade, and other trade items through the posts. At this time, the Dogribs, led by Edzo, were defending their territories from the Yellowknife Indians, led by Akaitcho. They also were defending their southern border from the Crees.[4]

With the development of the fur trade in the Northwest Territories, the Dogrib economy changed to one of cash plus subsistence, which resulted in fundamental changes in the trapping customs and the productive roles of men and women. Men dominated the cash economy, while both men and women continued to work within the subsistence economies. The disempowerment of both women and men as a result of contact is discussed more fully in the text and in the Reflections on Selected Literature (pp. 111–32).

The first missionaries arrived in the Ft. Rae area about 1852. The overlay between Dene belief systems and Christian ones was extensive. Initially, in the early contact period, it seems that both became entwined and included many similar interpretations of the world and its Creator and spiritual events. However, with the eventual establishment of Catholic institutions, such as the church and the residential school, socialization by non-Dene created a conflict with Dene socialization and, in fact, removed the children from the continuity of generations and oral traditions.

At the time of contact, the Dene had a well-functioning social and political system, which included an understanding of how their world worked and how intertwined the human world was with the spiritual and physical ones. Balances were essential in Dene traditional times and were maintained through the application of a rigid system of rules, which were passed down orally through many generations. The rules taught the ways of behaving "properly" so that people could survive in what was essentially a very harsh environment. The rules centred on the group's harmony within itself and with the "other" worlds of plants, animals, and spirits. Individual rights were secondary.

With settlement in communities, less mobility, and the arrival of non-Dene into the Dogrib region, life became more complex. Dogrib rules were not followed by non-Dene traders, nurses, missionaries, and the RCMP. Rather, these non-Dene began to impose their ways and laws on the Dogrib people. This overlay sometimes "fit" within the Dogrib belief

---

4 See Helm and Gillespie (1981) for a full account of Dogrib history.

system, its rules for living properly and its political system. However, the Dogrib social, political, religious, and economic systems began to weaken with the imposed non-Dene ways of doing things. Changes began to take place inevitably affecting the Dogrib ways of doing things. Adaptations took place all too quickly and soon many Dogrib ways were not being passed down to the next generation. Some were forgotten; some were retained.

The importance of the collectivity and the need for all individuals to contribute to the well-being of the group, to be governed by consensus and protected through harmonious balances, began to erode. The ultimate results are evident in contemporary Dogrib society in which the balances no longer exist. Individual rights and needs come before collective ones, leadership is elected and consensus is no longer the process of governing. Non-Dene functionaries and institutions hold the balance of power and continue to erode Dene ways. One such major institution is the non-Dene justice system.

This research seeks to identify the traditional Dogrib justice system, which is still remembered in considerable part by the elders, in order to assess whether the ways of doing things in the past can be relevant and practical for the present. Its goal is to determine, if the non-Dene overlay were removed, whether the Dogrib system might be revived and useful.

We turn now to the research process, findings, and recommendations.[5]

Starting up: The Dene Justice Project

In 1988, the NWT Minister of Justice, Michael Ballantyne, asked the Dene Cultural Institute (DCI) if it would like to participate in a training program for aboriginal justices of the peace (JP). After consulting with elders and the members of the Board, DCI declined to participate in the JP training but instead proposed that research be done on traditional justice systems so that any changes now would be based on traditional knowledge and experience. The Minister agreed to support such research and later provided start-up funds for the project.

The proposed research was discussed by DCI at the Dene General Assembly in 1989. The Chief of Lac La Martre indicated his community would be interested in having the research take place there. DCI then contacted the Arctic Institute of North America (AINA) to determine whether I might be available to work with the Lac La Martre people on this project. I agreed, not only because of interest in the topic, but also

---

5   This brief history is discussed more fully in Reflections on Selected Literature on pp. 111–32.

because it would mean a return to the community after an absence of thirty-two years![6]

Initial discussions with the Lac La Martre Chief, the Band and Hamlet Councils were held in the fall of 1990 attended by DCI, AINA and GNWT Justice representatives. After formal approval for the project was obtained from the community leadership, discussions focused on the criteria for selecting the Community Advisory Committee (CAC) and Dogrib researchers to train for the project, both of which were community responsibilities.

Looking for funding

Aggie Brockman (DCI) and Joan Ryan (AINA) then began to raise funds for the work. GNWT Justice had offered start-up funds and we approached Justice Canada to match those, asked Canada Employment and Immigration (Dene-Metis Training Group) for funding for the training portion of the project and approached various others agencies. A major funding request was submitted to the Social Sciences and Humanities Research Council (SSHRC). At this time, we also invited people from relevant agencies and funding agencies to sit on a Technical Advisory Committee, which would keep the project relevant and on track.

Aggie Brockman and myself moved to the community in January 1991, having chosen to start the training program even though complete funding was not yet fully in place. The training program ran from January until June. In May, we were informed that our SSHRC major funding proposal was successful. We were also told that "we had fallen through all the cracks" and they were happy we had survived the review process! This is an important point since we were doing community-based research, were not an academic unit, did not have graduate students involved, and the research would not necessarily result in a scholarly publication. However, the relevance of the project and its participatory methodology appealed to the Council, which then saw fit to grant us funding. This flexibility is noteworthy and efforts should continue to encourage Council members to fund participatory action research (PAR).

---

6 I was in Lac La Martre in 1957 for four months and in 1958 for six months as a community development teacher. I taught basic literacy, started the school program, helped people put in gardens and outhouses and hauled logs for the housing program. Dogs were tied up, a dump started and there was public health education to try to end the annual epidemic of dysentery. I also had an "outreach" HBC with basic supplies in my cabin. I went on to establish similar summer programs in other Dene communities and in the Eastern Arctic. I have fond memories of the Lac La Martre people of that time, my canoe trip to Ft. Rae, and the dog team trip to Yellowknife.

The fact that I was well known to Council and had done credible and scholarly applied work in the past was helpful.

Other funding came in slowly from Federal Justice and GNWT Culture and Communications. We also used some core funds from DCI and AINA to cover expenses during the proposal writing and consultations processes. Once secure in the knowledge that the project would be funded over three years, we moved into full operation.

Selecting the CAC

Criteria for selection of CAC members were arrived at by the Band Council by consensus; they required that the elders be a majority, that the Hamlet and Youth Group have some representation on it, and that the committee be chaired by the Chief. The importance of having a good CAC had been established in the Gwich'in Project.[7] The work of the CAC is vital in maintaining community control of the project and making sure that all major decisions are made by consensus.

The work of the CAC included selecting staff for training and research, monitoring the project, establishing personnel policies, meeting regularly with staff and the principal investigator (PI) and the project director (PD) to discuss concepts and terminology being used in interviews, reviewing difficulties arising during interviews, helping staff with unfamiliar terms, verifying results, and, in general, just being supportive. Our CAC did all those things and gave 110 percent to the project. Any CAC is a tremendous source of support and energy when working well, which ours did. It was not always pleasant work for them.

Selecting research staff

The first task of the CAC was to review applications from local people wanting to work on the project. Criteria established for staff selection included: respect for the elders, willingness to work with elders, fluency in both Dogrib and English, ability to read and write English, reliability, and the willingness to commit to the project for the two-year training and research period.

I also asked that the CAC choose men and women for the team, based on the premise that women might talk to women better about some things that only women experience, such as pregnancy and childbirth. This

---

7 The Gwich'in project included setting up a Language and Cultural Centre and the training program for a pilot project on Dene medicine, which tested and established that PAR worked in the NWT.

premise turned out to be only partly true; regardless, it is still my experience that a combination of men and women make a better balanced research team than one composed of only men or only women.

These criteria turned out to be the first item of negotiation! It was clear when the PI and PD arrived back in the community for the selection process that decisions had already been made. Although we had no vote on these matters, we did expect that candidates would be interviewed and that we would be able to ask them some questions. Not so! The CAC had decided!

However, as a courtesy to us, they asked the people they had chosen to come to meet with the CAC. They had chosen three men. We pointed out that we required women as well, a point which they had agreed to earlier. They then asked that we hire a fourth person who would be a woman! We did a quick budget run-through and decided we could manage. The CAC explained to us that they had chosen the "best" people for the job; not only did they meet the criteria, but they also had more schooling than others who had applied.[8] We had some doubts about the men, given their past patchwork work records. It was the first challenge of PAR and we proceeded in good faith and with good will.

Participatory action research methodology

PAR is a process whereby all members of the team share power, responsibility, and decision-making and co-operate fully to make sure the goals of the project are realized. It is not an easy process and the group's interaction has to be negotiated so that there is true sharing of power in all matters.[9] PAR works only by consensus.

In the Lac La Martre case, problems began almost immediately. The PI and PD and one research trainee were women. There were three men, none of whom initially wanted to work with the woman chosen by the CAC. Two of the men held very high opinions of themselves and their knowledge; one of the men was in a position of power on Hamlet Council. Two of the men had assault records, and one was being sued for child support. All of the men were alcoholics and had not been able to

---

8   The level of achievement in schooling is not a PAR concern, provided basic English literacy is in place. In fact, people with little schooling often know their traditions better than those who have been "out" to school; they also often have higher fluency in their own language and more respect for it.

9   See Ryan and Robinson (1992).

hold jobs. The woman was a highly respected member of the community and very active in church work.[10]

On the positive side, all were fluent in Dogrib. One of the men had taught the Dogrib language in the school and had some experience in reading and writing Dogrib. One man had been a radio announcer and felt he had the skills to do interviews.

PAR stresses that the facilitator focuses primarily on individual positives so that a group strength evolves. Through considerable opening up of communication in the beginning, it is possible to assist people to look at the positives, to arrive at consensus when decisions have to be made, and to reduce the need to be competitive or to assume authority and power, rather than to share it. This was our task!

Using the strength of the man who had taught in the school, we asked him to be our Dogrib literacy instructor. He agreed but wanted more money than others were receiving. The others agreed he could be paid more for the literacy training period but would then be cut back to the same salary as other trainees for the research work.

The man who was on Hamlet Council wanted the project to pay him while he was at meetings, often several times a week. We negotiated an agreement which allowed any member of the team to provide some community service, on project time and money, for a day or two a month.

We were forced by a court order to withhold the wages of the man who was being sued for child support. This led to much discussion within the group about the traditional and current responsibilities that men have in family matters. It was a discussion that would arise many times in the context of other externally imposed sanctions on the men.

These problems created discussions within CAC as well. Did the project have a responsibility to the community to allow time off for community service, i.e., Hamlet Council? How were we to handle the imposed external legal requirements (the garnishee) when we were attempting to document and legitimate traditional ways of dealing with such matters? How much "action" is implied by PAR in these things? Did the community want to take any responsibility for negotiating a more culturally sensitive way of handling the child support issue?

There were also problems for the PI and PD, strangers in the community, but being well received and establishing friendships and acceptance.

---

10 These characteristics are not unique to Lac La Martre; in small communities men often have similar backgrounds and fewer women have been involved with crime and alcohol. In the current traditional governance project at Rae Lakes, elders refused to pick any men as researchers and in the Gwich'in project, the CAC picked five women and one man.

How could we balance our feminism and our advocacy in the context of working with the staff that the CAC had picked? Not unlike many women's experience, we were "silenced." We needed to keep the work on course even at the cost of some stress to ourselves. We tried to reduce the stress by writing personal notes for ourselves, by removing ourselves from the community when the abuse of women triggered by alcohol would be at its worst, for example, at New Year's and during the Winter Festival.[11] Eventually, we found comfort in our Dogrib friends who provided good food, good company, and good will.

The CAC established a policy, after several absences by the men that they forgave, that any future absences due to alcohol abuse would not be accepted. The first absence would be dealt with by the PI or PD after consultation with the team, with a warning letter which would be put on file. The second absence would be reported to the CAC, some of whom would talk with the individual, and a second written warning would be given. The third absence would be dealt with by the CAC and would result in dismissal from the project. We did have some "excused" absences such as time to take children to the doctor or dentist, community holidays, special events and, of course, in the case of deaths.

A few months short of the first year and well into the research, the men unraveled. One went to jail in June after being convicted on an assault charge and was fired by the CAC. The second man was fired in October and the third was fired by the CAC in November, both for alcohol-related absences from the project. All had received warnings. None had been able to make the commitment required.

Quite apart from our personal sadness about the self-abuse, the termination decisions were devastating to the project even though they were long overdue. We each felt a great sense of loss because, in spite of the many difficulties, we had established a semblance of group action, acceptance, and loyalty. Further, we now were left with one staff person and needed to start training others again, knowing that we had neither the time nor the money to provide the comprehensive training we had provided the others.

Once again, notices were posted and people submitted applications. And once again, we learned before the interview meeting whom people favoured! The CAC selected a young woman, Diane Romie, and a

---

11 The PD had a home and spouse in Yellowknife, and she was able to get home regularly. The PI lived in Lac La Martre for eight months in year one and for six months in year two and considered Lac La Martre home for that time.

younger man, Lawrence Nitsiza, thus reversing the ratio of women to men to two to one.[12] Diane had been reared by grandparents and spoke Dogrib well. Lawrence understood Dogrib and could speak it but without the fluency of the older people. The CAC had selected him because he had expressed interest in going to college, and they thought he should have a stronger background in his own culture before leaving the community. He did go to college with more confidence and pride than he might have had otherwise.

The above commentary should make it clear that PAR is a commitment to a way of doing things that is decided in the community and that reasons for choices aren't always made clear in the beginning. In later conversations about the first three men, CAC members told us that the men had the skills and interest and that they had hoped the project would help them avoid further pitfalls of alcoholism. This belief that people can just make a decision to end their abuse of alcohol and "shape up," which we shared from time to frustrating time, reminded us that we have to shift ideas and accept the fact that alcoholism is a disease out of control of the individual until he or she makes himself or herself available for treatment.

In fact, we did bring in an alcohol treatment team for staff to meet with, we helped them establish a support group, and we vacated the house one night a week so they could meet there. Trainees were encouraged to bring their families to work to see what they were doing and to get a feel for its importance. The men were offered the opportunity to go to a treatment centre and were assured by CAC that they would continue to receive their salaries for their month away. One made application but then did not go.

Apart from the obvious lessons learned about the need for staff to be reliable, it is clear that the personal costs to others in the project and the financial costs in terms of time lost, additional CAC meetings to deal with the problems, and additional time costs for training new staff must all be included when considering who is the "best" person to participate in PAR projects. Sobriety thus becomes an additional and critical criterion for PAR research staff selection.

We include the above record of difficulties in our discussions because PAR tends to be highly successful in most cases and its pitfalls and de-

---

12 An interesting action of the CAC was that they interviewed Mike Romie, Diane's husband, to ensure he understood what would be involved if she took the job and to assure themselves that he would not be jealous of the fact that she was earning money.

mands are seldom documented. Indeed, at the end of this project it remains the research method of choice because it transfers marketable skills, increases individual confidence, enhances self-image and allows people to define who they are from a position of strength. The two women trained on our DJP project are translating and doing computer entry at the same time. They were the researchers for the Dene Medicine Project and worked quite confidently on their own, with minimal assistance from the PI and PD for that project.

PAR takes time, energy, money and commitment. In order for the process to work, the PI and PD have to commit to at least three years on the project. If we were to add proposal and report writing to the process, it would extend project time to between four and five years and would be the weakest component of the community process since most community people have little interest or skills for preparing proposals or (scholarly) reports for funding agencies. Even the PIs and PDs have great difficulty meeting funding agencies' criteria and deadlines.

However, we did encourage staff to write quarterly reports, and they were required to report in Dogrib to the CAC at its regular meetings. They were also required to translate for the PI and PD, when needed. Much of the discussion at the CAC meetings was done in the Dogrib langauge, and we requested summaries only at the end of extended discussions. This process creates a neat system for returning local language discussions to the CAC and community, and most elders are delighted to have young people speak Dogrib to them. It takes time for the younger people to accept the fact that the elders appreciate their efforts and will not laugh at errors or when they find they don't know the "old" words. Once this trust is established, conversation starts and, by year two of the project, we usually do not have an extra interpreter available since our own staff feel competent and comfortable doing the translation on most occasions. These are the "pay-offs" of PAR.

While this may seem a long explanation of PAR in the context of the Dene Justice Project, it is important to understand why these projects take so much time and money. PAR involves the whole community, provides training, which leaves expertise in the community, and obtains rich data, which are verified on a regional basis and therefore are more reliable. The data are obtained in the language of the community, and therefore we get more information, and more people get a bit of money. Finally, the research report summaries appear in all the Dene languages and the main report has wider circulation than most research reports. PAR also tends to create requests in other communities for similar research and therefore increases local knowledge, expertise, income, and interest.

Marie Adele Rabesca translating tapes
in the Dene Justice Project office, 1991.

Lawrence Nitsiza and Aggie Brockman entering data, 1991.

The training program

The Lac La Martre comprehensive training program ran from mid-January 1991, to June 1991; further on-the-job training continued throughout the life of the project. Training consisted of:

1. The Dogrib literacy program, which enabled people to learn to read and write the standardized Dene alphabet. This portion of the training was done by Francis Zoe, who had been the Dogrib language teacher at the community school in Lac La Martre. As well, there were workshops, one of which was provided by Ron Cleary, the Dene linguist trainee from the GNWT Language Bureau; the second was done by Betty Harnum, formerly of Justice, then manager of the GNWT legal interpreter training program. A further workshop was done by Lucy Lafferty from the Dogrib Divisional Board Learning Centre. The workshops were opened to the community and approximately six additional community people attended. All were enjoyed by the trainees, who were very excited about learning to read and write in their own language. As well, we sent tape translations and transcriptions to the Language Bureau, to Lucy Lafferty, and to two independent language consultants in order to assess the trainees' accuracy and the level of language skills being acquired. The feedback was very useful and allowed people to correct persistent errors.

Language development continued throughout the project. Unfortunately, the two trainees taken on at project mid-point were not able to have the same level of Dogrib literacy training, but they were assisted by Marie Adele Rabesca, and they do know how to use the Dene font on the computer. They continued to upgrade their language skills as workshops in the region became available. Initially, literacy training took the full morning. Later, it was reduced to individual and/or group work for about an hour a day and attendance at the occasional workshop.

Given the difficulties spelled out earlier, transcribing each interview into Dogrib was abandoned and staff concentrated on Dogrib to English translation.

2. Translation skills were developed throughout the project and provided an opportunity for people to upgrade their English writing skills. This was done by some general teaching time in which common errors were noted and worked on, for example verb tense and plurals. As well, individual consultations took place daily in order to help staff improve their written translations.

Finally, in order to ensure accuracy of translation, each translation was reviewed by another staff person. Staff also reviewed external translators' work. If "old" terms were used by elders, sometimes staff did not understand them, and they kept a file, as well as posting them on the bulletin board. Unsuspecting elders dropping in for tea were asked to help explain and translate the terms. This process increased Dogrib vocabulary and the number of unknown terms became fewer as time went on.

3. English upgrading was accomplished, as mentioned above, by reviewing translations with individuals. This helped identify specific errors. As well, staff were asked to read one hour a day and to write a summary of major articles they had read. We were not successful in getting people to read books, although some started. They did read local papers, such as the Native Press, News North, etc. Additionally, people were asked to prepare their work summaries for the CAC and TAC, which they themselves presented in both languages. Two written school presentations were done on the project, one to the Dogrib Divisional Board of Education. As well, staff were asked to take notes while attending court and to present them in writing for review by the PI or PD. English skills improved immensely.

4. Technical training included handling of recording equipment and learning to work on the computer. Aggie did all the technical training because of her considerable past experience as a reporter for Canadian Broadcasting Corporation (CBC). Tape recorders were of professional quality, and she was able to help people learn how to use them and the lapel microphones, and to keep batteries charged and equipment in good shape. Aggie spent considerable time with staff showing them how to get archival quality tape recordings of elders, and doing practice interviews.

After an initial computer orientation workshop done by Tony Clements of Arctic College, Aggie taught most of the computer data entry, showing people how to set up files, use the Dene font, and run a spellcheck. Now researchers are able to translate directly on the computer, a skill that was a long time coming but which has been achieved with competency and pride.

Also, Aggie set up a system for filing and managing the master tapes. Two copies were dubbed; one went to the school storage room for safekeeping, and the other went to external translators. Translations were also duplicated with one copy accompanying the tape to the school and one going on file after review. It took an inordinate amount of time to keep the tapes going in and out for translation but all were completed by January 1993.

5. Research methodology for using open-ended interview guidelines was handled primarily by myself. Practice interviews were done with people who were not elders before any "real" ones were done. Interview guides were developed with the CAC and some other elders from time to time. Initially, each staff person discussed their interviews on return to the office, problems were identified and the group arrived at solutions and helped each other with difficult terms, etc. The main problem, at first, was to get staff to ask one question instead of three at one time and to help them think it through before they went for the interview so that they could explore topics fully. Researchers had most difficulty creating follow-up questions after the elders' responded and tended to move to a new topic. This eventually was corrected but not as fully as desirable. The whole group would discuss the outcomes of interviews in the initial stages to make sure we were using the right terms and concepts. Part way through the first set of interviews on natural resources, we had to change the term "laws" to "rules for the right way of doing things" because researchers determined that they were not getting relevant responses using the specific term. When they changed the term, on the advice of the CAC, they got more information and more relevant answers. This made us realize how important it is to have precise and correct terminology and to keep checking concepts and terminology with the CAC.

Developing the interview guidelines

Developing the guidelines for each set of rules was a complex process and took many meetings with the CAC. The process was:

1. Staff discussed ideas, concepts and content which should be asked about in the specific unit, i.e., rules for maintaining relationships between the natural environment, animals, plants, and humans. Key Dogrib terms were agreed upon by the Dogrib researchers. Specific terms and concepts about which to ask elders were identified. Any points of disagreement or uncertainty awaited the next CAC meeting for resolution.

2. Much discussion took place about the culturally appropriate ways of asking for information. As well, we discussed whether some matters should be discussed only with men and others dealt with only by women. We tried to identify which items might be sensitive and which might be asked of anyone without offence. We also discussed which of the items Aggie or I had raised should be dropped and which of those we suggested could be included appropriately.

3. The next step was to draw up the list of Dogrib terms and concepts on topics for interviews in Dogrib and English. I asked for literal translations of the Dogrib, so I could be assured that the concept was correct, as well as the term. Going back and forth between languages took considerable time and effort. However, this was the most important part of evolving the interview guide and the Dogrib researchers learned a lot from the elders while the PI and PD learned the many differences in conceptual thinking and phrasing. It was an exciting process.

Sophie Williah, member of the
Community Advisory Committee.

Johnny Bishop, member of the Community Advisory Committee,
with Joe Zoe Fish.

4. We then met with the CAC elders and talked in general about the type of information we thought we should have, and the concepts and terms we had come up with. Elders discussed each of the terms, changing some and adding others. They then approved the list and agreed that we could proceed with the interviews. Although the issue of male/female sensitivities was raised with each unit, elders did not feel that there were things only men or only women could discuss and urged us to ask for that information from all elders.

5. Elders helped us to draw up a list of the most knowledgeable people on the particular topic for interviews. The Dogrib researchers took turns selecting people with whom they most wanted to work. Selection was not based on the sex of the interviewer or interviewee, but rather on relationship and friendship. And then the work began.

6. Each researcher did five interviews and then we re-evaluated the guidelines. We met with CAC to review difficulties in terms or content. Following this process, things went fairly smoothly, except in a few cases. In one case, the elder being interviewed chose to talk scripture rather than to respond to the request for specific information. She was dropped from the next round of interviews. Some people were too deaf or ill to take part. Only one man refused to be interviewed because he felt it was not worthwhile to talk about what used to be.[13] In a few cases, researchers decided to switch people on their list, that is exchange them with each other, and this usually solved any interpersonal problems that arose. Probably one of the most evident problems was when interviewers touched on topics that the elder thought the researcher should know. This created some gaps in the information because researchers felt foolish asking obvious things or got answers like, "you know that, why are you asking?"

At one point, researchers felt they weren't getting any information about family violence and they didn't want to pursue it because they were uncomfortable both about the topic and the inappropriateness of asking people to talk about things they didn't want to talk about. We held a meeting of all the elders involved in the project and simply asked them what the problems were in talking about these matters, whether they would respond, and whether we were asking inappropriate questions. After a lengthy discussion in Dogrib, there was agreement among the elders that the researchers could come and talk to them again

---

13 Interestingly, this man and his wife volunteered to be part of the Medicine Project, which followed.

about these matters. Later, in discussions with staff, they reported that people were uncomfortable because they did not want to discuss such personal matters until they were more confident about confidentiality. There may also have been an age factor here too, which made the elders feel somewhat hesitant to discuss such problems with younger people.

Observing at court

The purpose of attending the non-Dene court was to see how things were handled, how different judges approached the same matters, what types of charges were being laid, how those charged acted and responded, what types of judgments were made and how they were followed, and what, if any, participation there was by the Chief and Council, parents and the community. It also permitted trainees to take notes and to see where they perceived or missed things. Court attendance also provided a useful cross-cultural assessment because Aggie and I noted things differently than did the Dogrib researchers. For example, we tended to react more to the lack of translation, whereas the Dogrib people tended to feel that if translation was provided properly, it was a bonus. As well, we were outraged by the treatment of a young woman by one lawyer in a sexual assault case, whereas the Dogrib women seemed to feel that she had put herself in that position, i.e., exposed herself to public scrutiny and attack by men and deserved no support from women. This certainly was a major difference in our views and one which arose in the context of the research on many occasions.

As things turned out, there were significant differences between the behaviour of judges and between the Territorial and Federal Court processes, especially with regard to interaction with community members, the court set-up and the nature of the judgments. This was also true of the legal-aid lawyers and the Crown attorney. Occasionally, the Crown counsel came in a day before the court rather than flying on the court officers' plane. During the time of the project, a decision was made by the Chief Prosecutor to have the same Crown counsel attend each Territorial Court in the community. This helped community members get to know him, and people began to feel free to ask questions and to call on him for advice.

The legal-aid lawyers changed regularly and they and the native court worker came with the court party on the plane. This meant clients had very little time with their lawyers since the rest of the court party waited while they met. This put people under tremendous pressure. Often the native court worker did not come at all. On one occasion, we observed the legal-aid worker as she stood in the doorway of Council Chambers and shouted across twenty people to the defendant, "Are you pleading guilty?" The quality of legal-aid services in Lac La Martre can be described as minimal at best, and often as dismal.

These observations raised questions about the inequities of providing quality legal service to aboriginal peoples. No one doubts the integrity and commitment of legal-aid and native court workers. However, it is clear that the time allowed with clients is far too short to provide adequate counseling services or to obtain adequate legal advice. On most occasions, the lawyers spent about five to ten minutes with each client while the court party waited to begin the day's work. When the Crown counsel was able to come in the day before court, discussions were much more productive, and the complexity of some cases became apparent.

During the project, Chief Zoe asked the Territorial Court to allow the community to deal with a major theft. He also asked the Supreme Court to allow the community to deal with a custody case. These cases will be discussed later in full detail. For the moment, it is sufficient to say these requests were out of line with project timing, well ahead of the community organization needed to determine which cases to deal with, and well ahead of the establishment of a group of responsible people to follow through on any decisons made.

These "unanticipated" consequences of participatory action research projects often occur because people can begin to see where they want to go and even if things aren't in place, they move on an *ad hoc* basis – often to the detriment of community negotiations. Usually, they move before things are in place, and too fast. The result is they then have to backtrack.[14] Because some people move ahead without being properly prepared to act on the basis of consensus, others follow, and then the level of miscommunication, confusion and irritation becomes extensive.

For example, one Territorial judge said all juvenile cases could be turned over to the community, assuming that the Dene Justice Project would take this responsibility because he misunderstood our mandate and assumed the CAC/DJP was the "justice committee."[15] The next judge who came in wouldn't allow any community participation, not even the moving of chairs so elders could hear. He also made derogatory remarks about the community not having a justice committee and commented

---

14 As in the Apple–Bishop custody case, when Marie Adele had to rewrite her affidavit, with the advice of the CAC, discussed fully later in this report.

15 Some communities have established "justice committees" to advise the Court about the accused and his/her disposition; they also oversee community service sentences in some communities. Lac La Martre does not have a justice committee of any type in place at this time.

that the previous judgments (by another judge) for youth community service were worth nothing in that no one was supervising the youth. On several occasions, one judge referred to the Dene Justice Project as the "justice committee," and, on one occasion, ordered us to attend a community meeting, document it, list names of participants, record the decision, and report to him in writing at the next court. We did this because it was an "order," but we were not happy to be put in this position by the court, which did not even ask if such an action would be within our mandate. We usually take our orders from the community only, and those are based on consensus.

Attending court was useful because it led to many discussions about how things might have been done differently had the Dogrib people handled those cases themselves.

Great bitterness and hostility was expressed by the CAC members, and some community people, about what they perceived to be continuous unfair jailing of people for non-payment of fines.

We also heard from several people that testifying against a community member was very hurtful to the person who was required to testify because it was so culturally inappropriate to denounce someone publicly when they were present without arriving at some mutually agreeable remedy. And, of course, there arose many discussions about the strange concept of "not guilty."

From my own perspective, I found the court process to be uneven, ranging from heavy-handed and arrogant to concerned and sensitive. I am particularly concerned about the community service judgments since in the absence of a Dogrib justice committee and a youth supervisor, they make a mockery of the system.[16] I am also concerned about the shifting attitudes of judges, with one bringing an interpreter and earphones, seating elders where they could see and hear, adjourning for community consultation, etc., while another won't even allow chairs to be set in a circle and court tables placed so people can hear. The lack of a regular and trained interpreter and the use of local people who often misinterpret, according to the Dogrib staff, is also alarming. Finally, like some of the Lac La Martre people, I find it incredible that someone can go to jail for non-payment of a fine while a man who sexually assaulted a fifteen-year-old woman received a sentence of one day in jail (not served) and a thirty-five-dollar fine.

---

16 Since 1994, the untrained non-Dene social worker has taken on these responsibilities.

However, this "unevenness" also occurs in the community. While many Lac La Martre people were united in their determination to keep a female baby in Lac La Martre and argued loudly that they wanted to preempt the Supreme Court custody process, the same people have done nothing, although they have known about a sixteen-year-old who has allegedly been sexually abused since she was eleven years old. Further, the stepfather's lawyer screamed at her in the pretrial hearing, loudly announcing all her sexual involvements of the past, her pregnancies with different partners, and accusing her of soliciting her stepfather's sexual attentions. At the pretrial hearing, she was fifteen years old.

Contradictions of this type have serious implications for working out a Dogrib community justice system or even for "adaptations" of the non-Dene system that would make justice more culturally appropriate. Clearly, there must be considerable thought and education done on both sides.

Attending conferences

It is an important function of our PAR projects to expose staff to a broader audience and to help them prepare conference presentations. This serves several purposes: it provides information about what we are doing and why, how and to what purpose; it provides Dogrib staff an opportunity to present their work and to get to know others who may be doing similar work; it enhances the confidence of staff once they know how well re-garded their research is. Their presentations are generally vey well received.

Staff attended and presented at several conferences:

1. The Aboriginal Language Conference, organized by DCI in Yellowknife, was the first attended by the DJP staff. They were there to learn and did not make a presentation.

2. The Western Judicial Education Workshop, also held in Yellowknife, invited the CAC and project staff to attend and participate. Presentations were done by the elders, and Dogrib research staff participated as resource people in small group discussions with judges. Reaction from the judges was positive, although there were some questions raised about the relevance of traditional knowledge to the contemporary legal process. Some judges felt that traditional knowledge would not be useful because it had not been codified and because times have changed so much for aboriginal people. Others felt that the non-aboriginal system is far superior to anything else that could possibly be "adapted." These reflections will be addressed in the analysis of the Dogrib data.

3. The Northern Justice Conference was held in Sitka, Alaska, and we were offered three seats on the GNWT Justice chartered flight. The Chief, Marie Adele, and I were to attend. However, the tragic accidental death of Marie Adele's son just hours before departure dictated the return of the Chief to Lac La Martre. Chief Zoe asked me to go to Sitka anyway and to do the presentation that had been prepared jointly.[17] I did, and it was well received.

4. The Aboriginal Conference on Justice in Whitehorse was attended by Chief Zoe, Aggie Brockman, and Francis Zoe. The Dene Justice Project presentation was well received but had serious competition for attendance due to the tabling of the Manitoba Justice Enquiry at the same time.

5. The Canadian Anthropology Society meetings in Montreal were attended by Aggie Brockman, Marie Adele Rabesca, Diane Romie, and myself from the DJP; by Rosie Firth and Effie Blake from the Gwich'in Project, and by Martha Johnson and Bella T'selie from the Ft. Good Hope Traditional Environmental Knowledge Project. Jane Henson reported for the land-use planning group from the MacKenzie Delta and from the Oji-Cree of Northern Ontario. The day-long workshop on traditional knowledge and PAR, which was attended by sixty-five people, was chaired by Ethel Blondin, MP for the western Arctic. It was a great success.

6. Judge Douglas Campbell, director of the Western Judicial Education Centre, visited Lac La Martre with his family for three days and met with the CAC and staff, as did Norma Wikkler, a sociologist involved in judicial education.

7. Marie Adele Rabesca and I attended a Deh Cho regional conference on justice in Ft. Simpson and were honoured by the hosts with the gift of a beautiful book about Nahanni country.

All of these experiences contributed to the experience of staff, increased knowledge about the project and made staff feel they were making an important contribution to knowledge and to the people of Denendeh. It also led to an increase in self-confidence and to more comfortable public presentations for Dogrib staff.

We turn now to the presentation of our research findings.

---

17 It was PAR/DJP policy that the non-Dene team members do not present at conferences without Dene colleagues also presenting, unless there are unusual circumstances.

2

"Doing Things the Right Way: The Way You Were Taught"

Rules for Stewardship and Maintaining Relationships Among People, Animals, Plants, and the Spirits

The traditional setting

In traditional times, people lived out in their hunting/trapping territories most of the year. The camp groups were small, consisting of two
to four families. They gathered in larger groups in summer for fishing
and for treaty payments, and after missionization they gathered for
Christmas and sometimes Easter.

The usual camp groups were made up of relatives – often a man and
his son(s) and their spouses and children. Or two brothers or first cousins
might form partnerships and take their families out to the same camp.
Men hunted away from camp, leaving women and young children to
their own tasks while they awaited the return of the hunters with food
and hides. Absences ranged from one week to several. Sometimes when
game was scarce, hunters would walk great distances in search of moose,
caribou, and bear.

Elders reported that sometimes life was "poor"; there was little food,
especially if the men had gone a long distance. Some families had dogs
to move them from camp to camp, but the teams were seldom taken
when men were tracking game. They would, however, return to camp
for the dogs if they had cached meat some distance from camp. In these

23

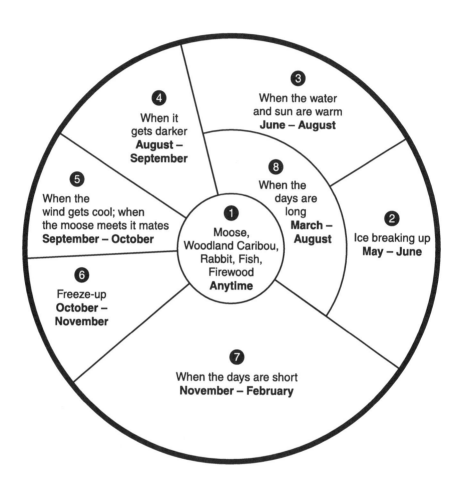

Dogrib Seasonal Round

1. All times of the year
- hunting moose and woodland caribou
- setting rabbit snares
- fishing
- gathering wood

2. Ice breaking up time (May - June)
- hunting porcupine, beaver and bear
- trapping muskrats for food and fur
- hunting grouse and ptarmigan
- fishing for dryfish
- cutting and peeling logs
- trading and visiting settlements
- collecting birch bark for baskets and canoes
- making paddles

3. When the water and sun are warm (June - August)
- hunting bear
- hunting birds
- fishing for dryfish
- gathering plants, roots, berries, spruce gum, tamarack bark
- tanning hides
- making hide teepees
- building canoes
- making blankets with feathers
- travelling and trading

4. When it gets darker (August - September)
- hunting barrenland caribou
- fishing for dryfish and stickfish
- making drymeat
- gathering berries, plants, roots, firewood
- tanning hides
- preparing to move out to camp

5. When the wind gets cold; when the moose meets its mate (September - October)
- hunting bear
- hunting ducks
- gathering berries
- tanning hides
- making clothing
- make snowshows, toboggans, toboggan bags and dog harnesses
- move to camp for trapping

6. Freeze-up (October - November)
- trapping squirrel, weasel, mink, fox, wolf, lynx, wolverine, beaver, martin, otter
- making sprucewood and babiche ice scoops for scooping out ice holes for nets

7. When the days are short (November - February)
- hunting barrenland caribou
- trapping
- hunting ptarmigan
- travelling by dogs
- making trails by snowshow
- sewing clothing with rabbit fur
- spiritual gatherings

8. When the days are long (March - July)
- hunting barrenland caribou
- trapping muskrats
- hunting ptarmigan
- ice fishing (with hooks)

small groups, children learned by observation and by being carefully taught. They had little opportunity to misbehave because adults were always there. Similarly, it would have been very difficult for adults to do wrong things because everyone would have known immediately. Therefore, little breaking of the rules in traditional times is reported by Lac La Martre people.

Social control was maintained both by consensus and by threat of serious punishment or consequences, such as shunning or banishment, if rules were broken. If these "balances" are understood, then it becomes clear that, in the case of a wrongdoing, there was considerable pressure to restore harmony as soon as possible between individuals and/or groups because survival depended on co-operation.

People shared beliefs and views about their natural world. They understood the interdependent relationships between themselves and animals, and they knew that different species relied on the availability of others for food. A balance had to be maintained in the interest of survival and therefore no imbalance created by over-harvesting was acceptable. They believed that humans, animals, and indeed all physical things in the environment have a life force and must be respected. Appropriate rituals had to be performed if animals were to allow themselves to be "taken." If the rules were broken, there was an inevitable and certain outcome: the group would suffer. What, then, were the rules and what were the consequences if they were broken? The Dogrib researchers interviewed thirty elders for a total of forty-seven interviews on hunting, trapping, fishing, and gathering. As well, the CAC provided information in meetings and verified findings at the end of the resource unit interviews.

What did we ask?

The guidelines for interviews were designed for open-ended and flexible discussions. Elders were encouraged to tell stories about living in the bush, their seasonal activities, gatherings, happy and unhappy experiences. Specific terminology was provided by the CAC and Dogrib researchers. The general categories for the interviews were:

Hunting: 1) What preparations and rituals were done prior to the hunt; 2) How were partnerships formed and ended; 3) How were territories defined and shared; 4) How was work shared between men and women; 5) How were game, fish, and furs shared; 6) How was knowledge passed down; 7) How was meat handled and how was it shared; 8) How were special parts handled, e.g., moose bell or fetus; 9) What were the rules for hunting "properly"; 10) What happened if rules were broken; 11) Who enforced the rules and who dealt with people who broke them; 12) How were resources kept in a viable state?

Trapping: The same questions were asked, but there were additional questions about partners sharing income and what happened if furs were stolen from a trap line.

Fishing: Approximately the same questions were asked, with one additional question about sharing income from sales to traders and others.

Gathering: Additional questions were added and addressed issues of responsibility for collecting and using plants for curing.

The data

General findings fall into several categories: stewardship, rules for handling game, special rules for women, partnership rules, sharing rules, food distribution rules, rules for sharing knowledge, and rules for use of special animal parts and plants for healing.

Stewardship

Stewardship, that is the responsibility to maintain the balance of land-use, hunting and trapping with the availability of resources so as to ensure a viable environment for the future, was the key factor in the hunting and trapping economy. The basic rule was to take only what was needed, in

> Our grandparents had a great deal of respect for the animals. That is why they lived well off the land and the wildlife. That is how it used to be.
>
> (AF, 10 August 1991)

a respectful way. Long before the Department of Renewable Resources was put in place, the Dene maintained their traditional territories well because they understood the fragile balance between the life cycle and the availability of food. The animals were not only game to be taken for food, fur, and hides; they also had a life force.

The notion of stewardship comes through clearly in all the interviews. Men consulted with each other about where to hunt, where animals might be found and how they might be approached. Sometimes, a person with special spiritual power would be asked to advise hunters about where game might be. A series of preparations, both spiritual and physical, took place prior to moving out to hunt and trap. Both women and men had responsibilities with regard to the hunt.

Women had the responsibility to make sure men were properly clothed and had food for the journey. When women accompanied men and stayed out on the land all winter, women also hunted, trapped, and worked on meat. An added responsibility for women was to make sure they did not affect the trails of animals or hunters by walking on them when they were menstruating or bleeding immediately after childbirth. The belief was that woman's blood had strong power which could affect others adversely.

Both men and women had responsibilities to make sure that young children did not disturb the hunt by being noisy and that they learned the skills for survival out on the land well.

> A woman's blood could draw strength away from a hunter.
>
> (MMN, 22 May 1991)
>
> Look at how I'm working with the [wood, fur, meat] this way. Watch so in the future, for you to live, you'll know how to do this. Pay attention and watch the details on how I work.
>
> (HR, 10 March 1991)

The spiritual connection between the life force of animals and humans was an important one. The hunter depended on this connection to lead him to the game, and the animal reciprocated by "allowing" itself to be taken. There were rules to be followed in the hunt, and if they were broken, the animals would not allow themselves to be taken and the lives of individuals would be at risk because they would have no food. Every individual had a responsibility to behave "the right way" with regard to animals and their spirits.

Rules for hunting big game (moose, caribou, and bear)

Men and young boys stalked big game. They had to approach quietly and even removed clothing that might rustle or catch on dry twigs. Snowshoes were covered in rabbit fur once fresh tracks were found so no sound could be heard. The hunters understood that moose had a keen sense of smell and hearing. Younger men and small children were left behind by the senior men once fresh tracks appeared, because they did not know yet how to walk quietly enough (JZF, 5 December 1991).

Once shot, the animal was left alone for a short period of time. There were two explanations for this: 1) so the spirit could find its way back to its own place with other game, and 2) so the meat could "rest" and it would taste better (PN, 3 October 1991). "Good" hunters used only one shell and had to be skilled marksmen. This was not only because shells were scarce but because it was important not to wound an animal, thus making it suffer. Nor was it acceptable to "club" animals who were wounded.

Women could not step over meat, blood or hunting gear. Menstruating women could not handle blood. Pubescent girls could not handle meat or blood. A woman's blood could draw strength away from a hunter even when he was on the trail and she was in camp. The animals also knew when a woman stepped over game or gear and would be affected enough not to allow themselves to be taken (MMN, 2 October 1991).[1]

When moose were killed, the bell was hung in a tree so other game would know that it had been handled "properly" and taken with thanks. Moose would then return to that area to be taken again. After a kill, butchering proceeded. No parts could be left on the ground. If camp was set up and dry meat made, bones could not be fed to dogs or put in the fire; they had to be covered by rocks or put in trees so the moose or caribou might reclaim them for its next life. If these rules were not followed, the animal would be offended and would not return to the area (JZF, 3 October 1991).[2] Blood was handled carefully since it represented the life force of the animal. It could be used for soup that only elderly men and women could eat. On return to camp, all meat was handed into the tent from the rear and placed on the man's side to avoid any possible contact with menstruating women.

Meat had to be shared. It was up to the hunter who made the kill to decide to whom he would give meat. Relatives and widows came first, then those who were considered "poor." If there was not enough meat to distribute, a feast was held for everyone. If several animals were shot both distribution and a feast were expected.

If a bear had been shot, the head was put on a stump, with a stick holding its mouth open, facing the winter sun. This ritual showed respect

---

1 The concept of "contamination" of trails and gear by women's blood is popular in the ethnographic literature on hunting and trapping societies. A more accurate term might be "endanger," which reflects a women's power to affect men's ability to hunt, thus endangering the survival of the group. Therefore, women had to learn to control their power. The concept of animals being "offered" relates to the need for women to control their power through disciplined behaviour so the balance between animals, humans, and the spiritual world is maintained.

2 Some of these practices continue today, and there is an effort in the community to teach young hunters how to treat caribou with respect. For example, recently, the chief hired two young men to clear the ice of caribou remains, and there has been some discussion of teaching younger people to hunt "properly" in the coming years. In 1992, the caribou came right into the community before migrating north again. The elders and chief asked people not to shoot them as the caribou were just reaffirming their relationship with people and would return next year.

Summer fish camp, Lac La Martre.

Winter fish rack, Lac La Martre.

for the bear which is credited with holding considerable power over hunters. If the ritual was done properly, the hunter would continue to be successful (AF, 24 May 1991).

Trapping

As with hunting, men chose partners with whom to go out on the trap lines. Occasionally, a man and his wife might be "partners" by themselves out on the land. Some women also had partnerships with their fathers and reported they worked "just like a man." This was usually the case when a man had older daughters but no sons old enough to go out with him (RZF, 8 May 1991).

Most of the rules for hunting also apply to trapping. However, one senses a less intimate relationship between trappers and their small game since there are fewer rules reported for handling small game. The beaver is the exception. If a beaver lodge were opened in order to get the beaver, it had to be repaired properly in order to protect the young ones left inside.

There was a rule that small animals like lynx and muskrat still had to be treated "properly," that is humanely and with respect, or they could "break your luck" (BE, 19 September 1991).

There was also a rule that territories had to be shared. There were no rigid hunting and trapping boundaries, so one could meet other hunters and trappers on the trail from as far south as Ft. Providence and as far north as Ft. Good Hope. However, there was a concept of Dogrib "territory" that made it important for the Dogribs to "host" people from other Dene groups entering their area. This meant that the traveller was welcome to one's food and tent, and if he had dogs, they too were fed. There was a courtesy among trappers to let others know when they were crossing each other's lines.

As in hunting, if a trapper was not having good luck, he or she could seek spiritual assistance from a "gifted" person (AF, 14 August 1991).

Like other meat, game meat was shared among family but there was no requirement to hold a feast or to distribute meat if one succeeded at trapping. The senior men were the "boss of the furs" taken in their territories. Younger men or women trappers had to turn over their furs to the senior man with whom they were camping. If sons went out to trap alone on their father's trap line, they also gave him the furs on their return (AF, 14 August 1991).

Fishing

Most dry fish for families was put up in the spring while stick fish for winter dog food was done in the fall.

Marie Klugie, collecting medicine plants.

Rosalie Zoe Fish, collecting tamarack for medicine.

A person could take as much fish as they could process. Unlike the big and small game conservation, there was no concept of needing to conserve fish stocks, since they were so abundant.[3] Both men and women, and some youths, checked nets and worked with fish.

In traditional times, there were no sales of fish. Sales began with the arrival of the traders, RCMP, and the missionaries. They needed fish for their dogs. Fish continues to be sold now, whereas, until recently, the sale of game was prohibited by both Dogrib rules and non-Dene laws.

There were rules for the handling of fish: scales and guts had to be piled in one place, away from scavengers.

Gathering

Everyone had the right to gather berries in any area. However, this was most often the job of women and children.

The senior men and women also collected plants for healing. Gifts were left in appreciation of the earth's willingness to provide medicine. The gifts usually consisted of tobacco, matches, shells, and sometimes bannock. Most men and women knew how to use medicinal plants for everyday illnesses. However, if they didn't work, a person with a special "gift" was called to help cure the person who was ill.

What happened to the person who broke the rules?

Some people did not follow the rules and were dealt with in a variety of ways. Some offences were minor and some major. Minor offences were dealt with by the senior male within the small camps. Major ones required a gathering and a public admission of guilt, restitution, and a process of reconciliation.

A minor offence might be a small theft. For example, elders reported that when youths stole some bannock, they were ridiculed and shamed. The person from whom they stole would pin the bannock on their jackets and everyone in camp would know they had stolen it and would laugh at them. This was considered to be a "deterrent"; it was unlikely the youth would repeat his or her theft because they would not want to face ridicule again.

A more serious offence, but not a major one, would be the theft of an animal from a trap. This offence would be reported to the head man

---

3 There is no consensus on this. Some people said fish stocks were conserved in the same way as game. However, the majority of people said that they could take all the fish they needed for their families and dogs.

(*k'àowo*) in camp and he would then speak "harsh words" to the person who had stolen the fur. The thief would be asked to acknowledge his theft and to return the fur (or another of equal value) to the person from whom it had been stolen.

If the offender refused to do this, the senior people gathered and confronted him. He was placed in the centre of a circle and people gave him "harsh words" about his inappropriate actions. They demanded he acknowledge his guilt and promise to return the fur. This stressed the importance of restoring harmony within the community, reconciliation with the person he had offended and compensation through replacement of the fur. Once that was done, no further action was taken and no further mention of the offence was made.

Failure to behave properly, while on a hunt or while trapping, had serious consequences and was considered a serious offence. If a person mistreated an animal, for example by breaking its bones, no one would hunt or trap with him again. Nor would they provide him with meat. Such actions put the group at risk, a risk people were not willing to take. The offender would be shunned. This made life very difficult for him because it is extremely hard to hunt or trap without a partner. It is unclear from the accounts whether the individual was forgiven at some point. The discussions seem to indicate that the offender would have to move to another area in order to find a partner.

Similar consequences befell the individual who did not share his game in "poor" times. He also was shunned and could not find another hunting partner.

Summary

It is important to note the importance accorded relationships between people and game and the many rules which maintained that important interaction. The dependence of the Dogrib people on game for their survival underlies their world view and the rules for relating to the environment and game. The rules were taught carefully and enforced by senior men and women. Offences required immediate action designed to make sure the offence was not repeated. The action was public and required an admission of guilt. People knew when something wrong had been done, and they knew who had done it. In the small camp, it would have been difficult not to know. Still, guilt had to be admitted to the group.

Further, concepts of accepting personal responsibility for one's wrong action was central to the process of "judgment." However, the consequences were not designed to be punitive. Presumably, the public admission of guilt was in itself enough punishment. Emphasis was then placed on restoration of harmony since in small-scale societies it is important that people be able to live and work together without major conflict, especially when survival depends on cooperation, sharing, and viable partnerships for hunting and trapping.

Reconciliation was also part of the process, since harmony could not be restored until the wrong had been made right. This was usually straightforward since one had only to return what one had stolen, if it had been a theft.

In the case of offences against animals, it is not clear whether rituals could be performed to restore harmony between the human and animals. Since most accounts provided by the elders indicate that the person was shunned and had to move out of the small group, it seems that no resolution of these cases was possible.

Reconciliation was a key factor. Once harmony was restored by public acknowledgment of guilt and by returning the stolen article, reconciliation was achieved by ending the incident. That is, no further mention of the matter was made. This could be construed as "forgiveness."

Conclusions ✳

We see that the Dogrib had quite a clear system of justice in traditional hunting and trapping times. The component parts were:

1. There was a clear set of rules that were designed to maintain harmony within the society and between the natural, animal, and human worlds.

2. The rules were carefully taught by one generation to the next and enforced by daily instruction, observation, and expectations of proper behaviour.

3. Offences ranged from slight to major, the most serious being mistreatment of game.

4. The senior members of the group dealt with offences; they judged the offence and determined what remedial actions had to be taken.

5. In serious offences, there had to be public admission of guilt. The collective group was involved in speaking "harsh words" to the offender who had to explain his actions to them.

6. Once guilt was admitted and appropriate remedial actions were defined by the group, the individual had to restore harmony and reconcile with the person(s) he or she had offended.

7. Failure to comply resulted in shunning and, on occasion, banishment.

8. Once the offender had met all the instructions for restoration of harmony, restitution, and reconciliation, he or she was forgiven. That is, the incident was not mentioned again.

9. There was no concept of "not guilty," nor was there any way of "appealing" the judgment of the community.

10. While senior men and women took part in speaking harsh words, and in making decisions about remedial actions, all people in the community were present as observers and all adults could speak.

In the following chapter, we turn to the findings on "rules for living together," that is "family law," which addresses how children learned the rules (socialization), rules for marriage, rules for relationships between men and women, special rules for women, and how offences were dealt with.

Family[1] *Rules*

Rules for Living Together

The traditional setting

Extended families lived in bush camps most of the year. Traditionally, this could include a senior man and his adult sons and daughters with their spouses and children. People spent the winter hunting and trapping and gathered at the mouths of rivers for summer fishing. Later, with the arrival of the missionaries, they gathered at Ft. Rae for Christmas and Easter feasts. With the arrival of the fur traders, mainly Hudson's Bay Company factors, people made an annual trip to trade furs and to pick up supplies. About the same time, the RCMP established posts and people gathered in the larger centres for Treaty payments in July or August.

In the Dogrib area, Ft. Rae was the centre for the HBC, RCMP, and the RC Mission and Hospital. Until the late 1950s, the Lac La Martre people took their furs by canoe to Ft. Rae and were paid treaty there. The priest made journeys into Lac La Martre and some families went with dogs for winter gatherings in Ft. Rae.

---

1 This term means "extended" family, which includes in-laws.

Most activities were carried out under the guidance of a senior man who had expert skills in hunting and trapping, wisdom, and sometimes a "gift," that is, spiritual power. He was the "*yabahti*," which is sometimes translated as "big chief," but should not be confused with the elected chief [*kw'ati*] after Treaty 11 (1921) under the terms of the Indian Act. The *yabahti* had an assistant called a "*k'àowo*," who was referred to as the "head man" or the "chief's assistant." Each camp had a *k'àowo* and if he could not deal with issues arising from offensive behaviour, then he would take it to the larger gathering at which the *yabahti* would call the senior people together to deal with the matter.

People respected their *k'àowo* and followed his instructions since he was the most knowledgeable among the people in the camp. Not only did he have wisdom, but it was his responsibility to make sure life was as orderly and as good as possible. He also was responsible when times were tough; people relied on him to advise them when game was scarce because of his skilled experience as a hunter and trapper.

What did we ask?

The guidelines for interviews were developed with the CAC and designed for open-ended discussions. There were 98 family interviews done with a total of thirty-three elders who were asked to tell stories about how life was when they were growing up, where they lived, what they did during the day, and where they travelled. As well, elders were asked to comment on aspects of life that made them happy or sad. They were also asked to talk about marriage, work, childbirth, life as adults, and death.

The Life Cycle

While life cycles begin at birth and end with death, I wish to start with marriage which was the start of the family and therefore a reasonable place to begin discussing family rules for living together.

Living together

There were several ways in which people could live together in traditional times and several ways in which such arrangements were made. In some cases, women were promised to men at the time of their birth. After pubescence, they went to live with that man. These arrangements were made by the parents of the woman and the man, and the young people had no choice in the decisions. They were bound by their parents' decision.

If a young man made a young woman pregnant, he was required to marry her. This was rare because people lived in such small groups, and women were protected by their parents. Men were always held responsible if women became pregnant prior to marriage, that is, it was he who had to "stand in the circle" in front of the elders, and it was he who was forced to marry her. He could refuse, but then he had to support her and the child. If he refused, he was banished.

Young people seldom chose their own spouses, but women could refuse to marry a man who had been chosen for them. In general, both young men and women married the partners their parents had chosen. The marriage was acknowledged by the *yahbati*, the elders, and all community members.

After the arrival of the priest, the community acknowledgment continued, but the priest also performed a Catholic marriage ceremony whenever he came to the community.[2] Eventually, young men and women began to live together without any ceremony being performed nor any acknowledgment from the community.

There are also reports of some marriage "kidnappings." This happened when a man from another Dene group came into the community and took away a young woman without the consent of the *yabahti* or her parents, maybe even without her consent. It is not clear from the reports how this was allowed to happen since there are also accounts of fathers or *k'àowo* tracking down young males who had impregnated women and bringing them back to the community to face the elders. Such "kidnappings" may have taken place in time of raids or wars. People remember hearing about these incidents but don't recall the details.

Men asked men for women, that is, a man wishing to marry a certain woman would ask her father for her. The father would reply that it was up to the woman's mother. Parents had the right of first refusal if they did not want their daughter to marry the man asking for her. They did not have to consult with her. Women were not permitted to initiate marriage arrangements. When women were requested, they did not always want to marry the particular man. If the woman was the "last" in the family, her parents might pressure her into accepting since it meant she would be supported by another man, thus relieving the parents of that burden. Sometimes grandparents were also involved in the decision and urged the young woman to do as her elders told her.

If there was male competition over the same woman, then the two men worked hard for her father, and whoever worked the hardest "won" the woman.[3]

---

2 When the priest visited small communities, it was not unusual for him to baptize children, marry people, do first communions, say prayers for those already buried, etc.

3 One CAC elder told us this was how he "won" his wife.

Apart from the traditionally arranged marriage mentioned above, there was also another type of arrangement. Young men sometimes lived with adult couples and worked for or with the man. If the wife became pregnant and gave birth to a boy, the young man would leave the household. However, if the woman gave birth to a girl, then she was "promised" to the young man and he continued to live with them and married the girl when she became thirteen or fourteen years old.

The general preference was for people to marry within the Dogrib regional group, but first cousins could not marry. People believed such unions were dangerous and would cause death or serious illness. Since people were so transient, many marriages took place between members of the Dene Nation but of different tribes. In the Dogrib-Dogrib marriages, men normally moved into their wives' community but in a few instances, women moved to their husbands' camps. In the case of intertribal marriages, women usually went to their husbands' communities. Only a few people are reported to have married outside the Dene group, for example, to Inuit. Such marriage rules ensured the gene pool was varied enough to prevent significant rates of mental or physical abnormalities. Most importantly, marriage alliances within the Dene Nation kept the hunting and trapping territories within the boundaries of Denendeh and ensured tribal alliances in the event of raids and wars.

Marriages were confirmed by the *yabahti*, who offered the young people words of advice after which the couple went through the camp, shaking the hands of the elders who gave them "good" words. That evening, there was a feast. The advice given focused on the rules for "proper behaviour." The young man was told to love his wife, care for her, work hard for her, not to give her harsh words unless she had done something really wrong. Young women were told to sew well, cook well, to keep a clean and comfortable camp, to obey their husbands and to be extremely careful about menstrual blood.

Once a woman agreed to marry, there was joy in the community. Shouts of "*masi*" from the man's family indicated their happiness with the arrangement. Once acceptance was confirmed, the young man began to work for the woman's father, helping with wood and trapping and hunting. When they started to live together, it was usually in her parents' camp.

The young couple stayed in each of their own parents' camps until seven days after the feast, at which time they set up their own tent or moved into the house of her parents. The young couple was advised not to sleep together for a year – or until they wanted children. Women reported that they often did not sleep with their men for a year after the birth of a child.

Fathers handed over their daughters with "harsh" words that gave the husband permission to beat his wife "if she does not do her work properly" (PB, 13 December 1991). The interviews are full of accounts by women of how harshly they were treated by men, both fathers and husbands. The accounts also show how vulnerable and abandoned women felt because if they ran home to their parents, they were "chased back" by one or both parents to their husbands. Given that some of the women married as young as fourteen, it is understandable that they felt abandoned and hurt. In any event, it made clear that "men were the bosses of women" (JB, 9 January 1992). It also makes clear that spousal violence is not new within Dogrib culture. Although men were "allowed" to beat their wives and children, they were expected to use this right reasonably and the *k'àowo* would speak to men who were considered to be too abusive.[4]

Separation

There does not seem to have been any culturally acceptable cause for marital separation in traditional times, and the long-term marriages of current elders speak to this.

If couples were having difficulty "thinking alike" (MMN, 18 December 1993), they could seek advice from senior male and female relatives. If this didn't help, the *k'àowo* might counsel them. If this didn't resolve matters, then both were called before the elders and the *yahbati* and put in the circle and given advice by the elders. Normally, this helped them resolve the issues. Some separations were allowed if a male was too abusive. In this case, each spouse returned to his or her own family. Each took what little "gear" they had brought to the household. Young children always went with the mother; older male children could go with their fathers if they wanted to.

Couples could separate if the man committed adultery. As in the case of pregnancy prior to marriage, men were considered to blame if adultery took place. The punishment for adultery was banishment. The reasons for this are not clear unless all adulteries were with unmarried women. In any event, they were rare.

---

4 The abuse should be kept in the context of the times; our culture had similar practices then. Men were the "bosses"; men hit women who didn't do their exact bidding; men and women hit children – and so did nuns, priests and teachers. The old rule of "spare the rod and spoil the child" has barely been left behind in non-Dene cultures.

The *yahbati* and *k'àowo* were permitted two or more wives – that is, however many they could support. In such cases, the wives often were sisters. Women were not permitted to have more than one husband. Monfwi, the legendary chief, was reported to have had twelve wives.

Men who raped were banished. This was a rare event. The idea of rape within marriage was not known; the CAC and other interviewees indicated that part of a woman's responsibility as a wife was to be sexually available to her husband at any time.

A few men abandoned their families, and they were not permitted to return to their communities.

Having children

Children were always welcome – boys more than girls. If a newborn baby was male, a cry of joy went up in the camp and fathers delivered one stick of wood to each household. If it was a girl, fathers did nothing, but, in a few cases, grandmothers reported they delivered spruce boughs to female elders (EM, 16 March 1992).

If a birth took place in the hunting or fishing camp, women who had borne children helped with the delivery and tended to the woman and her baby. People believed if women who had no children were present at the birth, the birth would take longer. Men were not usually present in the birthing tent in the main camp because women were considered more knowledgeable in such matters.

Preparations for birth included setting up a bed of clean boughs with lots of moss on top for the woman to sit on. As well, a frame of logs was made for her to hang onto while she knelt to deliver. Women would also help her hang on so she could push with the contractions. One woman sat behind the birthing woman to catch the baby. This was usually a senior woman, and the baby "was born on her hands" (RZF, 14 January 1992). Once the baby arrived and the umbilical cord was cut, the baby was passed to one of the women to wipe and wrap and then she or he was put in the moss bag. The cord was kept by the maternal grand-mother until the next child was born or until the child was one year old, at which time the grandmother put it high in a tree. People believed the animal or bird who ate the cord became the guardian spirit of the child. Fine ash was used to heal the baby's navel and was applied each time the moss diaper was changed. Meanwhile, the placenta was delivered and the mother could rest.

Women who had just borne children had their own set of dishes and utensils and stayed on one side of the tent. They went out the side of the tent to a place of their own to void, and they were not permitted to walk around in the camp until their bleeding stopped.

Procedures for birthing differed for women out on the trail. When the woman started labour, the man would set up camp, including a separate place for her to give birth. He would attend to her. If they were a short distance from their camp, or that of another family, the man would help with the delivery and then would take the woman and baby on the sled to the camp. If they had no dogs, the man would walk ahead to camp and leave the woman and baby to follow, making her own trail, when she had rested. If she got cold, she made her own fire.

Obviously, birthing in camp was more comfortable for the mother and safer for the baby. Elders discouraged pregnant women near term from going out to hunt and trap with their husbands. However in cases where families were out all winter on the trap lines, some women would be on their own when giving birth.

Sometimes women died trying to give birth or for other reasons prior to the birth of the baby. In these cases, people report that the baby was "cut out" and kept alive if it was big enough. A female relative of the mother usually raised the baby as though he or she were her own (MAM, 7 January 1991). If a baby was stillborn, or born with any abnormalities, it was considered a bad omen and usually the mother was blamed for doing something wrong. Elders could not recall what these wrongs might have been.[5]

Given the preference for male children, one might expect accounts of female infanticides. People acknowledged they had heard such stories, but no one had any personal knowledge of infanticide. There is one account repeated in several interviews of a mother killing an older child by breaking her neck while shaking her in a rage, but nothing was done because it was considered to be an accident (EZN, 26 February 1992).

Raising children

Babies were well cared for by mothers and older female siblings. Men were not much involved in infant care but began to do things with their children when they began to walk. Nothing was expected of children until they "began to get smart," which was considered to be about four to five years of age. Prior to that, they were protected from danger by being tied with moosehide strings to keep them away from stoves and

---

5 Pregnancy taboos are well known for the Dene and usually include such things as not looking at people with spiritual power, not eating bear meat, etc. However, none of the elders could remember the specifics of many rules in any particular case. They did know that the pregnant woman had to have breached some rule if she delivered an abnormal child.

Elizabeth Zoe Nitsiza (top) and her mother, Mary Madelaine Nitsiza (right),
with (from left to right) Norma Ann Warren, Jennifer Moosenose
and April Nitsiza, Mary Madelaine's granddaughter.

Eric and Erica Gargan, celebrating Canada Day, 1992.

fires, out of the water, and away from tethered dogs. By age four, children were expected to walk on the trail so they could "grow strong" (BP, 6 March 1992). They also had their own chores, such as carrying one piece of wood into the tent. Between four and eight, children learned who their relatives were, took part in camp life, were tended by older brothers and sisters, and, generally, observed the activities of adults.

From eight years of age, children were expected to be functioning members of families. They had to bring in kindling, haul water and help with fish. Boys went out trapping and hunting with their fathers and learned how to be quiet on the trail, to walk long distances and not complain about cold or hunger. Girls stayed with their mothers in camp and learned how to sew, do fish, split wood, set nets, work on hides, and other such chores. They also tended small children.

By ten to twelve years of age, boys were expected to know how to set traps and snares, chop wood, and make fires. Girls went on the trap lines with their fathers if the family didn't have boys old enough to go. However, by the time of their first menses, they were considered too high a risk to take because they might not know how to handle blood "properly" yet. Once they had learned how to be "women," they usually married and went out with their husbands.

Both boys and girls were expected to help their elders. They hauled water and did wood for them, helped them walk if they were frail and took food to them. Children were taught they would live long lives if they respected and cared for their elders. All children were expected to obey and respect their parents and every other adult. Children who failed to move quickly when told to do something were hit on their feet or bottoms with a willow stick. If they were truly disobedient or disrespectful, they were not allowed to eat for a day. Although such discipline was harsh, it was considered necessary for survival that the child learn to do things the right way. They had to learn the rules so they would not endanger the group's survival through ignorance or disobedience.

The difference between discipline and abuse was determined by love and by the goal of teaching children to do things the right way. If parents loved their children, they would discipline them so they could learn well and have sufficient skills to live in a harsh environment. Abuse occurred when people did not care about the child and did not love her or him, when the action was done only to hurt, rather than to teach the child.

Elders sought to prevent children from disobeying their parents by telling them stories designed to frighten them. For example, stories about the Bush Man kidnapping children in the bush taught children to stay near camp. Stories also centred on tales of what the animals' responses would be if children disobeyed the rules. For example, if a menstruating woman walked over a hunter's trail, the animal would not allow itself to be taken and everyone would be hungry. Such stories registered with young people, reinforcing other instruction which had the main goal of teaching the rules for survival.

Pubescence

Young women were isolated at the time of their first menses. They stayed in spruce tipis made by themselves or their senior female relatives. This tipi might be close enough to the camp for sisters, mothers, and grand-mothers to visit, but far enough removed that it would not be near any hunters' trails. Some were farther away and then visiting was infrequent. Sometimes when the main camp moved, the young woman would follow a day later making her own camp until the adults settled and she could build another tipi. One women reported not being allowed to follow and being left alone at the original camp for as long as a year (MAM, 7 January 1991).

One of the goals of isolation was to make sure men were safe from the effects of female power, considered to be very strong and symbol-ized by blood. A women's blood could move game away from the area if she walked on their trails or on the hunters' trails. Even if blood were not handled properly when the woman was in camp and the man was on the trap line, the hunter/trapper could be affected negatively and would not get any game. This in turn could affect group survival. So, it was important that young women learn how to behave appropriately and follow the rules when they were bleeding so they would not harm the well-being of the group.

Another goal was to make the person "strong" by having her tend to all her own needs without help. She had to get her own water, wood, and boughs and keep her own fire going; she had to set nets and snares for food. If she were close to camp, she was expected to do wood for others and leave it outside where they could take it, and she was expected to sew for herself and others.

As well, young women were meant to use this time to connect with their spiritual side and to come to grips with their power. No women reported a female equivalent of the vision quest experienced by young men. However, in the cases of those young women visited regularly by grandmothers, they were exposed to stories and teachings about the spiritual world, the role of women, and the expectations of their society.

The decision as to when a young woman could leave the menstrual tipi was made by her senior women relatives and depended on where the main group was camping. Some women reported being on their own for three months, while several others were left for a year. Some women expressed strong feelings of abandonment, and only one said she was sad to leave her comfortable tipi to move back into the group. Prior to leaving her tipi, the young woman was given a new set of clothes, moccasins and gloves and was told to burn her old ones. Parents had to reset their tent prior to their daughter's return.

Once back in her parents' tent, the young woman was instructed to avoid men's eyes, including those of her father and brothers. She was not allowed to face men and was told to sit on her legs in the presence of men, i.e., she could not stretch her legs out if men were in the tent. In some cases, women were told not to speak to men, and none was permitted to "walk around" if they were bleeding. Women were considered marriageable on their return to the full camp from the menstrual tipis.

When boys' voices began to change and they assumed the role of men, they usually went off for a while to the trap line with their fathers, uncles, and brothers. While discipline might have been strict, and they had to learn how to do things "properly," they had warm tents, food, and company provided. They were not isolated except when they went alone on a spiritual quest for several nights.

The kill of a young man's first big game was celebrated and feasted. Eventually, when they left their fathers' tents for their own, or for those of their fathers-in-law, they essentially became "the boss of themselves" and of "their" women.

Both young men and women were "tied" by their grandmothers at the time of puberty. This meant they had moosehide strips tied to their ankles, waist, wrists and neck. This was to give them strength, courage, and wisdom and to protect them from evil spirits.

Adulthood

People lived out their lives in a seasonal rhythm, working hard to survive and suffering during times of scarce game.[6] The impression one receives from the stories is that life was well regulated by the senior members of the society under the direction of the *yahbati* and his *k'àowo*. People grew up under harsh rules, but rational ones, enforced by parents and grandparents who knew the hardships which could be expected if the rules were not followed. By the time young people married, they knew both the rules and the reasons for them; in general, they followed them. As adults, men made partnerships with other males and hunted and trapped with them and their families. Women supported each other in work and in spirit as well.

----

6 See the Dogrib Seasonal Round, pp. 24–25.

There were few serious wrongdoings reported in the interviews. Murder was virtually unknown (except for killing during raids and intertribal wars), rape was rare, and abandonment of families by men was also rare.

Death was well known. There are several reports of stillborn babies and some of babies dying shortly after birth. There are many more stories of people dying of injuries, disease, and hunger. When people died, it affected the whole community because relationships were close. There were no wills and little property. Spouses kept the property of the deceased and passed appropriate items to adult children, who some-times took on the roles of the departed family member. Sons and daughters received their father's and/or mother's tools, equipment for hunting, canoes, etc. Personal clothing was burned; occasionally a man's rifle was buried with him. The burning took place on the day of the burial, and it is reported that the smoke enabled the deceased person's soul to travel to a comfortable resting place.

There was some fun in adulthood as well. People talk about the enjoyment of summer fish and berry camps, of feasts, of festivities after the missionaries came and after Treaty. They spoke of jokes they played on each other and of the yearly spring shaman's games. And some reported the excitement of possibly seeing a Bush Man or of experiencing other happenings that were "extraordinary."

As people began to age, the elders were treated with respect and caring. No longer able to go on the trap lines or to walk long distances, elders began to enjoy the benefits of having raised many children who now brought them meat and fish, fresh boughs, and wood.

There was a balance – not always ideal because the death rate was high – but a balance nevertheless between people, the land, the animals, and the spirits. As long as the balance was maintained, life went on and people were relatively safe, healthy and active. The disruption of this balanced life cycle and seasonal round came from outside. With the arrival of non-Dene in Denendeh, life changed drastically and many imbalances came into play, which will be discussed in a later chapter.

Adoptions

Upon the death of a parent, or in a case where a woman could not raise her child, the adoption process was clear. The mother's female relatives had the responsibility and privilege of raising babies and small chil-dren. If a mother with children old enough to help their father died, a male child of ten or older might stay with the father while the younger ones went to the mother's relatives, usually to sisters, but occasionally to her parents.

Agreements were verbal and binding. Once a child had been given to a relative to raise, she or he became that person's child and was treated no differently than natural children. Since the community was small, everyone knew a child's family history, and relationships between children and their birth parents were encouraged. For example, a man whose wife died might leave their children with her sister for several years, then later he would take his male children on the trap line with him. Such arrangements gave children an extended family and a sense of security. No limits were placed on relationships. So even if mother's sister had raised her children, their natural fathers knew them, related to them, and some reclaimed them when they became youths. Children raised by relatives expressed no sense of being abandoned or unwanted by natural parents.

Summary

We see that the rules for marriage and raising children do not vary much from other societies (including our own) in traditional times. The fact these rules existed made it very easy for the Roman Catholic missionaries to overlay Canon laws on Dene ones and for the Canadian government to put theirs in place too. In many cases, they were amazingly similar in content, if not in practice.

The rules for living together as family were straightforward:

1. Marriages had to be arranged. They required the consent of parents and elders. Acknowledgment of the union had to be public.

2. Women belonged to their parents and had to be released by their fathers to other men, although husbands deferred to their wives' decisions when daughters were asked for.

3. Close relations (e.g., first cousins) were not permitted to marry.

4. Marriages consolidated political ties and reinforced and extended territorial boundaries.

5. Men were the "bosses" of women; women had to obey men.

6. Children belonged to women, but sons were accountable to their fathers, even when they became adults.

7. Men were accountable to the *yabahti* and elders for pregnancies prior to marriage, for rape and/or abandonment.

8. Women's roles were mainly reproductive and productive; they bore children, made camp, dried meat and fish, tanned hides, sewed them and cooked.

9. Men were allowed to hit women if there were "just" cause. A "just" cause was determined by community standards and related mainly to a woman's failure to equip and provide sufficiently for her husband's hunting and trapping trips. This was seen to affect the whole community.

10. Children could be physically punished by either parent in the interests of survival of the group. The emphasis was on teaching the right ways of doing things, as opposed to punishment.

11. Puberty rituals isolated young women more than men but provided same sex bonding groups for both young men and women.

12. Women were responsible for the safety of men, trails, and game, through control of their strong power symbolized by blood. There were many rules and rituals that they had to follow to make sure their blood did not negatively affect the survival of the group by reducing availability and take of game.

13. Separation of married partners was not culturally acceptable and was allowed only under rare circumstances. The decision was made by the *yahbati* in consultation with elders.

14. Orphaned children were adopted by their mother's relatives. Adoptions were accepted by community consensus once the child went to live in another household.

15. Children were taught by both parents and grandparents. It was important that all the rules be passed down.

16. Children were expected to follow the rules, especially as young adults, so no one would suffer.

17. Young people respected elders and cared for them.

18. The emphasis of the rules was on maintaining a "balance" between the human, natural, animal, plant, and spirit worlds.

In sum, these were "right ways" of doing things, rules for living together which regulated marriage, separation, reproduction, adoption, limits for discipline, rituals for safety, and socialization to ensure the continuity of the society. We turn now to the findings on how Dogrib society was governed in traditional times.

Living Politically
According to the Dene Ways

This chapter is centred on the traditional political organization of the Lac La Martre people in order to understand how Dene rules were made, who enforced them, and how they worked.

Methodology and guide

The methodology was changed for this unit because we were so far behind in the translation of the other units and funding was running out. The CAC agreed to the proposed changes and elders co-operated fully. Rather than interview individuals, we had two groups of men elders and two groups of women elders meet regularly to discuss issues already identified by the CAC as being appropriate for this section.

There were five members in each group. Each member had participated in earlier interviews on the resource and the family rules. The sessions were facilitated by Aggie Brockman and researchers Marie Adele Rabesca and Diane Romie. The nine sessions were taped and the Dogrib staff provided translation. The interviews took place in the summer of 1992.

Topics for discussion were selected, and the terminology was developed with the staff and the CAC, as they were for the other units. The guide included the following items:

1. Who made the rules?
2. Could they be changed? If so, how and by whom?
3. Were new rules made as things changed?
4. How were rules taught?
5. Who had the authority to make decisions when rules were broken?
6. How was the *yabahti* chosen? What was his job?
7. How was the *k'àowo* chosen? What was his job?
8. What was the job of the medicine person? How did people prepare for this position?
9. What was the job of the prophet? How did a person become one?
10. What was the job of the spiritual jester?
11. What was the job of the diviner? How did a person become one?
12. Were these roles hereditary?
13. What was the role of women in leadership and social control?
14. How did conflicts and wrongs get resolved among people?
15. What was done about threats to do wrong things?
16. What was the effect of medicine power in keeping people from doing things the wrong way?
17. Who participated in "judgments" of people in the circle?
18. When offenders were told what they had to do to make things right again, who made sure they did what they had been told?
19. What happened to people who did things wrong because they didn't have much intelligence or were mentally ill?
20. When did the rules begin to change as a result of outside influence?
21. Why did people continue to use traditional ways in some cases but turn offenders over to RCMP in other cases?
22. Why did the chiefs allow the RCMP and priests to take over their roles and power?

There were no significant differences in the information provided by the men's groups and the women's groups. Therefore, the general responses are provided and exceptions will be noted. It should be clear that the above questions were not asked in a question-answer situation. Rather, elders were encouraged to tell stories, discuss the points and arrive at a consensus on who had power and authority, how it was used, how control was maintained, and who was responsible for making sure that things happened in the right ways.

Learning the rules

It is clear that the rules were not written down but were passed down orally. The senior men and women in each camp were responsible for making sure people knew the rules and followed them. As mentioned earlier, minor offences were dealt with by the *k'àowo*, who was usually the most elderly male in the small camps. If the *k'àowo* could not handle the issue, resolution awaited the next major gathering when the offender would be put in the circle. That person would have to acknowledge his or her wrongdoing and would have to listen to harsh words from the *yabahti* and all the elders, male and female.

New rules were created as the need arose. "New rules were for when new things happened. People would make a decision and work on it" (2 July 1992; men).

Leadership meant responsibility, power and authority

The traditional leader *(yabahti)* had the most authority and power. We were told,

> Monfwi was a great chief. He was like the government for the people. In those days people really listened...; he was the head boss and the leader. Our ancestors were poor but they had good ways of living, of talking to people and giving advice and direction. (16 July 1992; women)

> Ewagha, the *k'àowo*, had really strong words. Before people would leave camp, he would give them advice to take care of each other. He would say that he doesn't want any bad news to come to him from their camps. (16 July 1992; women)

The *k'àowo* was the chief's helper. Each camp had a *k'àowo*. He would tell people what had to be done each day. People respected him and followed his instructions. Because of his leadership, people lived well off the land. He was responsible for making sure people had wood and game. The young people would work with him.

> People used to meet often, at the *yabahti*'s house or the *k'àowo*'s house. They would talk about how to live their lives. (21 July 1992; women)

Apparently, these daily discussions kept people on the right path and brought the best wisdom to problem-solving. People felt secure in the knowledge that their leaders would make life as good as possible for them. In return, the leaders were given respect and loyalty, and people did the work that had to be done.

Leadership positions were hereditary, in general. If the son of the *yabahti* or *k'àowo* had the necessary knowledge and skills to continue his

Diane Romie and Charlie Jim Nitsiza at Dogrib Literacy Workshop.

Marie Adele Rabesca and Diane Romie with elders
at Rae-Edzo verification meeting.

father's work, he was asked to do so. It was not an automatic decision, however. People discussed it at length, and if the young man was not suitable, another person would be chosen by the elders. In other words, the best person got the job.

Women never became *yabahti* or *k'àowo*, although senior women were in charge of the camps when men were away. They did get respect. They were in charge of their children when young and were in charge of their daughters for life. Men respected women's decisions in these areas. Women also had a say, if they chose to say something, when a person was in the circle because he or she had done something wrong.

The characteristics required of leaders were demanding. They needed to have excellent leadership skills and be good providers to deserve the respect of the people. The *yabahti* was perceived as having a "special gift," which did not make him a medicine man but meant he did have spiritual power. That meant he had greater abilities to do the work well because he had greater knowledge and experience. The *k'àowo* followed the *yabahti*'s instructions and did not need a special gift in order to lead in the smaller hunting and trapping camps.

Leaders had other special helpers

The men and women who had medicine power were able to help out in times of severe illness and when game was scarce. Such a person could find lost people, and he or she dealt with mental and physical illnesses. They were not considered "leaders" but rather were "specialists" within the group to deal with extraordinary events and problems. Most people with medicine power were men, but a few women also had this power. Power was acquired through dreaming and fasting alone in the bush. However, specific skills were passed down from the older medicine people to younger ones who experienced the dreams.

If power was misused, it was usually employed against an individual. Most elders indicated power was mainly used in positive ways but there were a few stories about "bad" medicine, that is, hurting someone with one's power. We also heard stories about some "bad" medicine actually causing deaths. Medicine "fighting" was rare but was certainly known. It is understandable that people with power were not only respected but feared. Medicine men and women also are reported to have used their power to obtain highly desired spouses (love medicine). People with power and "special gifts" are still active in the community today (15 July 1992; men).

The spiritual jester was another specialist in the community.[1] He, too, could cure people's illnesses, but he used his special gift only in summer. It seems this was a ritual event carried out after people gathered for the summer to fish. The jester would dress in caribou hides and mask or in a caribou head and would dance through the camp seeking people to cure. He also could tell people how long they would live. Young women were not allowed to watch the jester because they might disturb him, or their power might affect him, and then people would get sick (15 July 1992; men, and 16 July 1992; women).

The prophet was another specialist who could tell people what would happen in the future. Like the diviner, he could see where the game were and could communicate with them and call them into the hunting territories where they would allow themselves to be taken. Likewise, he could call back the soul of a person who was lost so the person could find his way back to the group.

Both the prophet and the diviner acquired their special gifts through dreaming and through an alliance with an animal helper. The prophet seems to have had broader power and knowledge than the diviner, whose main job was to find the animals when they were scarce. No mention was made of women in these roles, which isn't surprising because the activities centred around hunting activities.

All of these specialist roles were based on beliefs and behaviours that fit into the general understanding of how the natural and human worlds interacted, and how those relationships had to be maintained in harmony for the benefit of the community.

The "powers" of the specialists supported the power of the leaders and provided a spiritual authority for the enforcement of the rules and the responsibility of elders to make sure the next generation learned how to behave in the "right" ways. These checks and balances kept the community stable and therefore viable.

---

1 "Jester" may be a poor translation of the term "*dze kw'i*"; people used this English term and described his work as "playing games to get rid of sickness, or when a person was not doing well." The "games" played were ones which healed, e.g., putting a stick into a father's chest if the son was ill with a bad cough. This was a seasonal ritual only and did not compare to the curing done by the more regular activities of the medicine man. The roles did not overlap: the medicine man did not become the spring "jester." I suspect the term is not really translatable and that "jester" is an accommodation.

What happened when the rules were broken?

As mentioned earlier, there was a process in place to deal with people who broke the rules.

Minor offences often were dealt with by ridicule, that is by laughing and making fun of the individual's behaviour. Or people might shun a person for a while, that is no one would speak to him or her to get the message across that he or she had behaved in an offensive way.

All offences were considered within a specific context. For example, it was not theft if a person took someone's axe without asking, provided he needed it, and as long as it was returned within a reasonable time and in good condition. Nor was it theft to take food from a trapper's cache if one were on the trail and hungry. Again, the food had to be replaced by the borrower, then the matter was settled. Some issues required more ingenious solutions. One dog story shows this: Two men claimed the same dog as their own. The *k'àowo* talked at length with the men, each of whom continued to claim ownership. Finally, the *k'àowo* said he could not decide who the owner was, so he would shoot the dog. One man then said, "No! Don't shoot the dog. It is a good dog." The *k'àowo* then declared him the owner of the dog since he clearly cared about it and didn't want it shot (FZ, fall 1991).

When the *k'àowo* felt an offence was too serious to deal with himself, he would raise it at the next gathering, and the *yabahti* and senior men and women would put the offender in the circle. This process included the whole community. The offender was kept there until he or she admitted guilt, at which point the senior people and leadership would give the person "harsh words." These words usually restated the rules and how the person should have behaved. They also made reference to the harm done to individuals and/or the group. Once the harsh words were spoken, the gathering shifted to discussing how the individual might make things better. People arrived at consensus about what the person might do to restore harmony, compensate the victim, and end the matter.

When a solution was proposed, the offender agreed to do what the elders had indicated would make things right. If the person did not agree, then the gathering had to decide what the outcome of the refusal would be. For example, if a man had impregnated a woman, he was ordered to marry her and to do work for her father. If he refused, the gathering might decide that she could stay with her parents and he with his, but he still had to work for her father in order to provide for the woman and their child. If he agreed, then the matter was settled. If he refused, the general decision was that he must leave the community since he would not follow the rules. Banishment was rare because few young people had the courage, or lack of respect, to "break the words" of the elders.

The most serious offences were ones which endangered the survival of the group by breaking the rules about the right way to relate to and handle animals, especially big game. The next most serious offences seemed to be adultery and impregnating an unmarried woman because these actions caused serious disruptions in the camps. If these could not be resolved, then banishment was essentially a death sentence. A man who could not find a hunting partner because he had abused the rules for dealing with animals could not survive out on the land on his own for long. The man who committed sexual crimes against women would be in a similar position.

There were no accounts dealing with murders and, in fact, most "murders" mentioned in the stories seemed not to have been dealt with, such as the death of the child due to the mother's rage and abuse. One explanation for this failure to deal with murder may lie in the extraordinary and spiritually dangerous contexts in which they occurred. For example, deaths caused by medicine fighting were not considered to be the responsibility of any individual but were blamed on supernatural actions out of the control of ordinary humans.

One effective way of keeping people from committing offences is to create fear of the outcome if one is caught. In all our accounts, people said they feared the discipline of their parents, they feared the power of the *yabahtis*, they feared "harsh words," and they feared being put in the circle. When one balances this fear with respect for animals and leaders and the accepted importance of doing things in the right ways for the survival of the group, one understands that only a few people dared not to follow the rules. As well, the reality of being shamed by all those gathered if one ended up in the circle, caused many people to think seriously before committing an offence.

Change and transition

As long as people lived in small groups spread out over vast territories they controlled their own lives. Once non-Dene began coming into the traditional Dogrib territories, things began to change. These changes came slowly at first; some were barely noticed. Many changes were countered by strong *yabahtis*. As time went on, however, the changes took place more quickly, and the leaders were unable to stop the process. It is not possible here to go into the history of cultural, economic, social, and religious changes. However, we need to consider causes of the main initial changes in the Dene way of life:

1. The missionaries arrived in the late 1800s; they were Oblates of Mary Immaculate, members of the Roman Catholic Church. Most were from Belgium and were French-speaking. The Mission Hospital at Ft. Rae was built in 1940.
2. The first fur traders arrived in the 1790s; the Hudson's Bay Company post opened in 1852, and the Northern Trading Company came into Ft. Rae in 1890.
3. The RCMP, representing non-Dene government and Canadian law, arrived shortly after the Hudson's Bay post opened.
4. The Treaty was signed in 1921 and brought with it non-Dene people with their own laws, education, economics, settlement, and health institutions.
5. Major changes took place in the 1950s with the arrival of electricity in early 1950 in Ft. Rae (and later in other communities) and the opening of the connector road from Ft. Rae to the MacKenzie Highway in 1960.

The arrival of the priests did not create an immediate problem for the Dogrib people. These men learned the language, travelled with dogs and by boat to the various camps and lived off the land with the people. They respected the authority and power of the *yabahtis* and *k'àowos* even as they sought to change Dene religious beliefs and practices. The priests were welcomed by the Dogrib people; their religious teachings were not regarded to be in any major conflict with Dogrib traditional teachings. In fact, it was the compatibility of the teachings which enabled the priests to make their conversions so readily.

The changes were subtle. The Dogrib *yabahtis'* own acceptance of new practices allowed priests to take over some of their previous responsibilities. For example, after the recognition of a marriage by family heads, the elders and the leaders, young couples headed over to the priest for his blessing to complete the recognition of their marriage. This was no conflict, only an additional ritual. The messages from the priests had already been heard from the Dogrib leaders and elders: love your spouse, take good care of each other, have children, raise them well, stay together forever.

And, like the *yabahti*, the priest was deemed to have a "special gift" from God and, therefore, he claimed spiritual power and authority. It was understandable that in the absence of the Dogrib *yabahti* in the small camps, the priest could fulfill somewhat the same role when he visited by providing advice and direction, resolving some disputes and condemning certain acts and behaviour. Eventually, as the stronger

Dogrib *yabahtis* died and were replaced by elected chiefs (*k'wa'ti*), the position of the priests became stronger. People who were used to following the instructions of the great *yabahtis* now followed the instructions of the priest and trusted him to lead them in safe and reasonable directions.

And so over a short period of time, Catholic rules began to replace Dogrib rules and church rituals replaced Dogrib ones. While these replacements had some logic because of the overlap of their content, it also meant some significant Dogrib rules, beliefs, and actions were displaced. The Dogrib holistic view of the world as a balance between the natural, human, spiritual, and animal worlds changed to one in which humans were at the mercy of the supernatural world as portrayed in Catholic beliefs. As a result, the Dogrib world became unbalanced.

Further imbalances were created as the mission schools removed children from the teaching of parents and grandparents. Later, community schools forced families to become sedentary, so children could attend school. This meant hunters and trappers could not take their families with them to the bush. As a result, family relationships and the style of life changed; for example, male bonding between hunting and trapping partners sometimes became a more important relationship than spousal ones. As well, many youth were cut off from the important spiritual relationships on the land and from the teaching of the elders.

The arrival of the traders (mainly Hudson's Bay factors) meant a shift in economic activities from subsistence to cash for furs. This shift caused women's roles to change. Women still worked but no longer received recognition for their work, nor did they receive cash for it. For example, women still tanned furs and hides, but men received cash or credit at the trading posts for "their" furs. This eventually led to a change from the traditional economic sexual equality between men and women to male economic and social dominance.

The RCMP arrived just after the traders in the early 1800s. They came to assert Canadian sovereignty of northern territories. They, as well as the Canadian government, failed to recognize that Dene sovereignty was already in place. They brought ideas from a different culture about the right ways of doing things. The Dogrib *yabahtis* recognized them as people with authority and power. Even today, the term for RCMP officers, "*mola kwa'ti*" means "white man's chief." Again, since the Dogrib *yabahtis* could not be in all camps at once, visiting RCMP were asked for advice on conflicts and offences which the *k'àowo* couldn't resolve immediately. The RCMP imposed their own ways of doing things, that is, they applied the only thing they knew: white laws. Akin to the priests' process of taking over religion, education, and health, the RCMP began to take over the management of conflicts and the breaking of their laws. They assumed the Dogribs had no laws.

In 1921, the Dogrib leaders signed Treaty 11. Almost all the stories we recorded indicate that the leaders who signed believed that they were signing a peace treaty, agreeing to share responsibility for the steward-ship of the land, animals, and people. And it is clear that Monfwi, for one, understood he would remain in charge of his people and territories. He spent the rest of his life fighting the priests, the RCMP, and other non-Dene for control of decisions that affected the lives of his people.

The main outcome of the Treaty on the lives of people was in the change and manner of leadership. Under the Treaty and the Indian Act, chiefs were to be elected. At first, people continued to follow their own ways and to pick their own leaders, chosen by consensus when they had large gatherings. However, the rules had changed and, as a result, non-Dene functionaries took control over decisions, rules, breaches of rules, and socialization of children. They were challenged by the Dogrib leaders, but these challenges were not successful.

We asked the elders to tell us why this was allowed to happen. How did their own leaders' power and authority slip away, and why were their rules replaced with non-Dene ones? People said:

> The *yabahtis* had strong words ... they taught the people how to live. After they [*yabahtis*] all died, we had to have elections. These elected chiefs had no strong words. That is why the police could take over. When there were strong words, the people would listen to each other. (22 July 1992; women)

And further:

> The change [to elected leadership], people did not like it. When [name] accepted money for being chief, it affected a lot of things. Our land, our culture, our way of life changed. Before, when we had leaders who didn't get money, they had strong words and actions ... they did a marvelous job for the people (23 July 1992; women).

> Those who came from down south, I don't know why they took over. They didn't count [rely] on the chiefs; they ignored them. They did just what they wanted (July 23/92; women).

> We have had elections only recently.... They [the elders] are not satis-fied since the young people are running things because it is not in our ways....We haven't followed the traditional laws, maybe that is why it is hard to follow the Dene way [now] (5 August 1992; men).

> Since the RCMP have come, we have let everything go. Everything in our hands, we have let go. We have let the priest and the RCMP take over (15 July 1992; men).

Who are we afraid of today? Not even the chief because he doesn't put his words into action (15 July 1992; men).

While people are not always clear about how power and authority were taken away by non-Dene, they do feel it started with the arrival of non-Dene in the area, especially after Treaty, and they blame the imposition of the election of chiefs for major negative changes. They also recognize that the transfer of power came with the deaths of some of the more powerful *yabahtis*, such as Monfwi and, later, of younger *yabahtis* such as Jimmy Bruneau and Louis Beaulieu, both men who were very experienced and knowledgeable about their own culture and who had special "gifts."

These men were succeeded by younger elected ones, who were not fully experienced or knowledgeable in their own culture because they had been removed from the community to attend residential school. The schooling process, especially in residential schools, broke the educative and socialization processes of the elders. Also, residential schools almost always devalued the Dene culture, as nuns and priests attempted to erase the cultural practices and spiritual beliefs of the young people, as well as forbidding the use of their own languages. This devaluation of all things Dene was probably the single most devastating aspect of the Dene-non-Dene contact period. It ruptured the continuity between generations, ripped the social fabric of the local cultures and destroyed the vital balance between the human, animal, natural, and spiritual worlds.

Finally, the elders saw payment to chiefs as the final straw in the loss of the Dogrib ways of doing things. It should be noted also that the non-Dene government officials preferred to deal with male leaders who had some schooling. "Schooling" should never be equated with education, and does not equal or replace training in one's own culture. Nor was residential schooling a valuable or effective replacement for the Dene ways of doing things "the right way."

Summary

All rules were made by the elders who made their decisions by consensus; their decisions were based on experience and knowledge of the world in which they lived.

1. Rules were passed down from generation to generation by grandparents and parents. These oral traditions included stories about the supernatural world and how it worked, stories about how the animal world worked, stories about the disastrous outcomes when rules were broken.

2. There was direct teaching by one or both parents on specific rules for doing things the right way in daily life and in special times such as pubescence. Children also observed their parents' behaviour and learned to do things the same way. Children were punished for not doing things the right way and learned from their mistakes.

3. Rules were enforced by all adults and some adults had more power, authority, and special gifts to make that enforcement very strong. Leaders and specialists had the final authority and responsibility to make sure everything worked well, that the group survived and that things between the natural, spiritual, and human worlds were kept in balance.

4. New rules were created when circumstances changed, and there was a need for a change in rules or for totally new ones. These new rules were made by the *yabahti* and *k'àowo* in consultation with all the elders. They were discussed at length and then explained to the people. They worked hard at making them appropriate and enforceable.

5. Rules had a logic and consistency that made them a part of daily life and special events. The need to break the rules was infrequent and the motivation not to break them for fear of the outcome was very high.

6. People who had mental or physical handicaps that led them to break the rules because they didn't understand them were not put in the circle. Parents and relatives were responsible for making sure these few people were protected from the dangers of their own behaviour. They were under constant supervision.

7. Mechanisms put in place to help people not to break the rules included early teaching, storytelling, direct action, discipline, ridicule, shaming, shunning, harsh words, and banishment.

We can see that the Dene had a system of local government that provided strong leadership based on the rules for doing things the right way. These rules were arrived at by consensus and were passed down to the next generation in a variety of ways.

The definition of government usually includes a recognition of continuous leadership, a set of rules with which to govern, and a territory bounded by recognition that other groups also have territories. It also includes an identity, based on common ancestry and descent and which is recognized by those outside the group as well as by the group members.

The information provided in the preceding chapters proves clearly that the Dogrib people had a government and rules which they enforced for the common good.

The intrusion of non-Dene into Dene traditional territories and their challenges to local authority and institutions is well documented. As the elderly *yabahtis* passed away, and the younger, elected, partially schooled chiefs took over, the non-Dene were able to assert more and more power and control over the Dene. At the present time, that power and control can only be described as totally paralyzing the exercise of any Dene traditions, power, and control. It is appropriate, therefore, to turn to a discussion of how the Dogrib people might take back control of their lives, institutions, and cultural systems.

Įnę̀ę̀ Nàowoò Sìi Eda
Wet'a Ts'et'į ha
Kènahots'iìhde ha

5

Using the Past to Build a Better Future

**How can traditional knowledge return the society
to the Dene ways of doing things in the right way?**

The goal of the research was to find out if traditional knowledge about
Dene justice could suggest ways of dealing with social problems now.
The present chapter flows from discussions with Dogrib regional elders,
and is also based on the information we collected in Lac La Martre.
Throughout the time of the research, elders and others in the community
have said clearly that they wish to do things in traditional ways and that
they wish to "take back" control of their own lives and institutions.

These wishes tend to cluster around problems of social control in the
community, on the land, and on education and health issues. Only the
issues of social control are discussed here, but it is important to think of
"Dene Justice" in the context of non-Dene dominance in so many other
areas of Dene life. Not to do so would result in a lack of understanding
of how deeply people feel the need to take back control of their own
lives and to rebuild their own institutions. While these issues are dealt
with from another perspective in Reflections on Selected Literature
(pp. 111–32), the concerns of people are not academic. People want a

change; they think that, if they took back control, life would take a turn for the better for them and future generations.

In the same way as the non-Dene "justice" system is often far removed from any truly just action because of the legal manipulations of information, a Dogrib system will likely not be seen to be just until all community members can understand how traditional values could provide a sound basis on which to rebuild their system. It is not the purpose here to see what adaptations could make the non-Dene system more acceptable to the Dene. Rather, our goal is to explore what traditional values people can take forward upon which to build a current rational way of dealing with problems of social and personal control so the quality of life becomes better for everyone in the community. Needless to say, the practices will have to be culturally appropriate and acceptable to men and women, elders, and youth. Negotiations will take time and will require good will, an educative process, and the reaching of consensus.

What traditional values can we identify from the research?

Respect

In the past, one of the most important aspects of good relationships, good partnerships, and a good life was respect. Adults respected each other, younger people respected elders, children respected parents. Everyone respected the animal spirits, the *yabahtis* and *k'àowos*, the medicine people, and other spiritual specialists. Respect was taught early and became expected behaviour. In fact, respect is probably the primary value from which all others flowed because, without respect, the balance between people, the land, plants, animals, and spirits could not have been maintained.

Currently, people recognize there is little respect in the community. Elders are respected by a few (but certainly not by all) younger people. Chief and Council complain that people do not respect them, while others complain that Chief and Council do not behave in ways that merit respect. Children respect their parents in some cases, but not all. Some children and youth respect each other, but many do not. Some spouses have reasonable lives, but many do not have the mutual respect that would make life a little more peaceful. The question then becomes, how can respect be regained?

Moral and spiritual beliefs

In traditional times, there was a deep sense of morality based on spiritual connections with the animal world and an understanding of how human and animal worlds met at a spiritual level to ensure the survival of both. There was a major tradition of "connectedness" with spiritual forces which helped maintain human life. It was a partnership in which people respected and appreciated their animal guardians, and, in return, animals allowed themselves to be taken. As in most partnerships, this only continued if both partners acted "properly" – thus the many rules on how to treat game.

Roman Catholic beliefs and teachings altered these partnerships and, in many cases, replaced the connection to Dogrib spirits with those of Christian spirits. It is not useful here to ask whether this exchange was beneficial. For some, it has been, but the shift took many people into a spiritual void. Had the exchange been left at the spiritual level, that might have been workable. But with the added attacks on Dene culture through mission education and devaluation of all things Dene, the cultural connection broke and people were set adrift from their own cultural base and identity. As we noted earlier, the adoption of Catholicism was relatively easy because many of the Dogrib beliefs were so similar to Catholic ones. It is that Dogrib core of beliefs that people want to retrieve and reinstate now.

At the moment, neither Dogrib spiritual beliefs nor Catholic beliefs are being taught to young people in effective ways. Few young people attend church at all except on important feast days, such as Christmas and Easter. Fewer still are familiar with Dogrib beliefs and rituals.

At the moment, few young hunters have any holistic understanding of the environment and about the ways animals should be treated. Many older hunter/trappers have said that it hurts them to see caribou hunted by snowmobile and carcasses dropped in the back of trucks without even having been gutted or having the hides removed.

It would seem, then, that people could retrieve some of the values of respect and moral values by giving back elders their roles as storytellers, teachers, and advisors. Youths could be trained to hunt well and to treat animals and people properly.

What has this to do with returning to Dene "justice"? The research team and elders believe that people who are rooted in their own culture by understanding and knowledge, who are connected spiritually to the land, and who have some deep sense of a cultural self will assume more responsibility for their actions.

Self-discipline

The accounts by elders show that, in traditional times, roles and responsibilities were clear and that the majority of individuals were expected to behave properly. This required self-discipline. The harsh treatment of women who didn't do things "right" indicates that they were expected to learn their jobs and to do them properly. In the same way, children had their tasks and were expected to do them properly. The underlying belief for these expectations was that if everyone did their own jobs properly, the group would survive and prosper. Otherwise, everyone was in danger.

It is clear that few people wish to return to such harsh ways, or times. However, the fundamental underlying value of self-discipline, rather than discipline by others, could be taught now. One of the characteristics of life in the community now is the overwhelming lack of self-discipline and responsibility for self. Some children don't go to school, or if they do, they go late because parents aren't up. Some adults don't show up for work. Some young adults bully elderly parents. Spousal assault is common. No one takes responsibility for others. People break their own by-laws by bringing in liquor, drunken fights are common, and most contemporary "crime" takes place under the influence of alcohol.

How might pride and self-discipline be reclaimed? One way would be for people to take back responsibility for themselves – to sober up in a serious way, not just off and on. A program might be put in place to teach children how to take responsibility for their own lives regardless of what adults are doing. Everyone could learn again to respect themselves and the elders.

Self-reliance

In traditional times, people took pride in their skills. They had the security of knowing that they could cope alone in the bush, if need be. Both men and women understood that they had strength and competency. They made great efforts to pass these skills and knowledge to their children.

Self-reliance is not so noteworthy in current times. People have become so demoralized, and so colonized, they rely heavily on non-Dene for things they themselves could do. This dependency could be turned around if people decided to take back both power and responsibility for their own lives and for those of their children, and this would increase self-esteem and self-reliance. For example, leaders could insist that the school have Dogrib language immersion from Kindergarten to Grade 3 and Dogrib literacy throughout the rest of the grades. It is an official language and one that is still strong in the community. We know that people who use their own language have more cultural pride and a better sense of their own identity.

The Community Education Committee could also insist that every child have at least one week out on the land with competent hunter/ trappers, including some elders. They could reconnect with the spiritual and animal parts of their culture and learn how to treat animals properly.

They could listen to the elders stories and learn more about themselves. They could enhance their Dogrib language skills. They could gain confidence and learn that they can depend upon themselves and their own skills.

Similarly, leadership could insist that any non-Dene people or agencies coming into the community must use interpreters rather than always having the Dogrib people speak English. Many times English is used when Dogrib might be. Different perspectives might be acquired when non-Dene have to speak through interpreters; as well, such a simple act shifts the balance of power to the Dogrib people.

Sharing

In traditional times, people shared. They shared "things" like meat and fish, but they also shared knowledge, feelings, perceptions, and expertise. They shared thoughts about important matters as they met to discuss when to move camp, where to go, and how to find the animals.

This sharing was disrupted when the elective system was superimposed on people, leaving responsibility and power to a few men, rather than to the Dogrib community collective. People began to talk less about important things, and, with settlement in communities, families moved into permanent housing so there was less interaction among people.

Exchanging goods became less frequent as the cash economy grew. Another outcome of shifting from a subsistence economy to a cash one was that reciprocities could not be kept in balance. Game meat was once distributed to all, but groceries bought for cash at the store cannot be shared so readily. "Things" began to acquire a cash value, and those who had more buying power did not want, or could not afford, to share things they bought with cash.

So instead of everyone sharing whether things were plentiful or scarce, people began to accumulate. This also became the case with services. People asked for cash for services that in the past they got or did for free, based on their values of mutual sharing and caring. For example, younger people who went out to get wood used to bring some for the elders. Now, elders, or social services, pay for their wood, while most young people do nothing.

Sharing, respect, and caring were all linked together in the past as responsibilities for others. Now they are not. People could return to reciprocal giving and taking, if they chose to do so. For example, instead of elders paying for their wood, they could trade dry meat for wood. Or, young hunters could give elders meat and get some back dried. There are many ways that sharing could be reintroduced.

Knowledge and understanding

In the past, the society worked well because people had a shared understanding of how the world worked. Young people were taught those beliefs by parents and grandparents and important knowledge was passed down from generation to generation. By the time young people reached puberty, they understood their place in the group, their responsibilities and their importance. They also clearly understood what might happen if they did not follow the rules and continue to respect the environment, the leaders, and themselves.

Life now is not so clear. The dismal lack of social control, often expressed by alcohol abuse and assaults, provides clear signs that people are not anchored in functional ways in their own culture. The many impositions of non-Dene ideas and ways of doing things are not understood by many Dogrib people, even now. Schooling in the non-Dene system, with little reference to Dogrib customs and knowledge, has failed to educate children in ways that would allow them to take their place in either the Dene or the non-Dene society. Catholicism has broken the ties with Dene spirituality and replaced it with a compartmentalized view of the world, which often makes religion an irrelevant part of every day life. People do not see a role for themselves in either society. Jobs are scarce; skills even more so. Pride is hard to achieve, as is satisfaction with one's own place in the universe. Anger underlies many situations and is let loose by alcohol and followed by abuse of self and others.

How can people reclaim themselves, and control over their lives, in ways which would allow them to move forward with pride and dignity?

A circle process could be put in place for "healing" and understanding. Knowledge of the Dogrib worldview could be taught by elders. "Bonding" among men and among women, and between them, could be facilitated so a new sense of caring is developed that would cut into the isolation and despair expressed so often now. Youth and elders could sit together once again to learn about each other, to develop pride and a sense of purpose in Dogrib traditions. Life could be reinterpreted from a Dogrib perspective that would make it more meaningful.

Caring for each other

It is clear that in traditional times, people took responsibility for each other's well-being. The *yabahti* and *k'àowo* were responsible for "their" people. This caring was expressed by making sure people knew how to behave properly, that their hunts were successful, and that they could turn to either of the leaders for help at any time.

It seems such caring is not quite in place now. People feel isolated from each other, often expressing feelings that indicate that they don't feel cared for by spouses, parents, children, nor by leadership. There are complaints that the Chief and Council only act on their own behalf and are not accountable to the community. Leaders are often seen as acting inappropriately, especially when drinking. People sense a lack of strength and self-discipline in the leadership and in themselves. They tear themselves apart with gossip and sometimes jealousy. Nor do people feel "cared for" by the non-Dene people; they feel criticized and put down by the teachers, nurses, social workers, judges, and police.

How can people return to caring for themselves and for others? A healing process could be put in place to help people redevelop a strong sense of their own self-worth that would not be so vulnerable to attack by non-Dene evaluations. A program could be put in place to stop self-abuse by alcohol and abuse of others when using alcohol. Anger management could be learned.

Chief and Council could have some working sessions that would help them improve communication skills and administrative skills. Community meetings, held on a regular basis, could return a sense of control to all adults and youth because of their real participation in decision-making.

Adults could care for youth by taking on responsibility to become partners with them in addressing problem behaviour and by teaching them traditional knowledge and skills. Adults could look at partnerships again as a means of making sure that at least one other family is doing all right.

The circle could be put back in place so the community reclaims its role to take responsibility for the actions of people who have behaved improperly. "Harsh words" could be given once again to make sure people understand that doing things the wrong way is not acceptable, but harsh words could be tempered by offers of help to learn to do things in the right ways. Such a circle would work only if youth and elders developed respect for each other and if leaders are seen to be sober, responsible, and accountable to the community.

While some of the thoughts expressed above have merit and seem relatively simple to put in place, we should not be misled into believing the processes to accomplish all these goals are simple – or painless. They require a lot of personal thought, commitment, and consensus. The community will have to commit to changes as a group because it will not work if some people participate and others do not.

Proposals for starting this process on several levels at the same time are made in the last chapter of this book. Meanwhile, let us turn to an examination of how the community started to reclaim some responsibility in three legal cases:

1. a major theft to which Marie Rose Moosenose pleaded guilty;

2. a child custody case involving two young adults, Dolphus Apple from Rae Lakes and Tina Bishop from Lac La Martre;

3. a case involving the theft of marten pelts from the school.

Ị̀nę̀ę̀ Nàowoò Wet'à
Ts'atị̀ị̀ Ị̀lè Sìi Nats'èhchi ha
Ts'ị̀ị̀wǫ

Taking Back Control

Three Case Examples

There were two major cases, and one minor, for which the community decided to take responsibility during the life of the DJP. Both major cases were marked by conflict, and both led to some anguish. Both involved the DJP in spite of our clear indications to the court and chief that the cases, and local action, were not really within our mandate at the time.

The major cases were taken on before Lac La Martre people were really ready to deal with them and before they had reached consensus about them. Both cases stand as good examples of how the Dogrib people and the officers of the courts see things very differently. However, in the long run, people on all sides learned something from these experiences.

Case 1: Admitted theft of $27,000

In the spring of 1991, the Canada Post Corporation and Sears Canada, Inc. realized something was very wrong with the Lac La Martre cash-on-delivery (COD) parcel orders. People were receiving their orders, but Sears was not receiving its money. Sears sent notices to customers because the company thought they had not paid their bills. Some people paid twice; others insisted they had already paid the post office.

73

An official RCMP investigation began at the request of Canada Post, which had been informed that parcels had never arrived, and at the request of Sears, which was not receiving the money people claimed to have paid. Within a few weeks, RCMP Constable Les Dell charged Mary Rose Moosenose (MRM), the post mistress, with "theft over"; specifically, she was charged with stealing $27,000 from Canada Post.

As soon as the charges were laid, many of the elders indicated they did not want a young woman with small children to go to jail. They felt this would be too hard on her seven children. They asked what they had to do to deal with the case themselves. Younger people in the community immediately began to say that if MRM did not go to jail, they too would steal and ask not to go to jail. Calmer middle-aged people debated whether it made sense for MRM to go to jail. Most felt that, if she did not, a "wrong" message would be sent to young people. Some young people who had gone to jail for minor offences, such as non-payment of fines, felt it would not be "fair" if she did not serve time.

The Crown (through the decisions of Chief Prosecutor Don Avison, and later Crown Counsel Greg Francis) decided that if MRM chose to plead guilty, they would work with Defence Counsel and the community for an outcome satisfactory to the court and to the community.

After many delays, MRM entered a plea of guilty. Greg Francis, Crown Counsel, then started a series of meetings with MRM, her family, elders, and others. The first Defence Counsel (who changed twice during the process) was not enthusiastic about the community involvement and decision-making. He felt the case should be dealt with as usual and that MRM probably would get a lenient sentence in the non-Dene system since this was her first offence.

Meanwhile, the elders and Chief waited for MRM to acknowledge to them that she: 1) had stolen the money, and 2) wanted community help. As time went on, the elders and Chief began to get irritated about MRM's inability and/or refusal to talk to them. Crown Counsel also awaited a decision. MRM's relatives and friends urged her to decide whether she would go the elders' route or let the court decide her fate. MRM's hesitation seemed to arise from two sources: 1) She was not sure about the implications of dealing with the elders, rather than the court; nor was anyone else. 2) She was afraid to appear before the elders because she knew they would be very harsh with her.

Eventually, word came that MRM wanted to do things the elders' way. When Greg Francis came to Lac La Martre before the next scheduled court, the Chief asked if he and the elders could have a meeting following a DJP meeting with the elders on other projects. After our meeting with about thirty elders was finished, Greg Francis arrived and was introduced to the elders by the Chief. Joseph Moosenose left, and I assumed he did not wish to be present during the discussions about his wife. However, he returned shortly with MRM, who was given a seat in the circle of people. There was dead silence and much tension. Eventually, MRM began to speak. She said the things people were saying about her were true. She had taken the money. There was an audible sigh of relief, people looked up again and some wiped away tears, including MRM. MRM went on to say she was sorry for her theft and that she did not want to go to jail. She asked the elders to help her and told them she would do what they said.

The women elders then spoke. They gave her "harsh words," which were later summarized for us by the Dogrib researchers. Essentially, they said what she had done was wrong, that it brought shame to her family and to the community, and that she now had to face the community. They said they would help her and that they supported the idea that she not go to jail. She was instructed not to gamble, drink, or play bingo. She was told she should visit the elders and listen to their words about how to behave properly, how to care for her family, etc. She was also told she should start trying to pay the money back immediately. There was some discussion among all present whether the Hamlet should give her a job and send her salary directly to the Post Office to repay her theft.[1]

Greg Francis explained that the community would have to come up with a plan that would meet the court's standards for "punishment," "compensation," and "deterrence." Later, Aggie and I took issue with him about this because we felt that if the court was going to leave the case in the hands of the community, then they should use their own ways and criteria for handling the case. This difference in ideas about who should control the outcome of the case is a good example of how difficult it is for non-Dene authorities to give up power. Terms used by lawyers and judges, such as we'll "allow them" to do X or Y or "they must" meet the demands of the court, indicated all too clearly who was in charge. In the end, the outcome was a compromise: the community met with the court's requests and the court agreed, in major part, with the community's recommendation.

It was informative to watch the elders and MRM at the end of the first meeting. After the harsh words, and the statements of Greg Francis, the Crown Counsel, people began to file out past MRM. Every woman

---

1 This was not done since the Hamlet insurance had paid Sears long before the elders and the court decided the case.

Crown Prosecutor Greg Francis and Chief Isidore Zoe
discuss the Mary Rose Moosenose case with elders.

Joe Zoe Fish (left) and Sophie Williah (far right)
having tea with a visiting elder.

gave her a hug and a handshake. The men shook her hand. The process of reconciliation had begun.

While the process seemed to be straightforward and simple, it was not. MRM did not visit the elders or start to pay her debt back, nor did she stop playing cards or bingo. She was seen walking around at night, and when people tried to talk to her, she took off in her truck to avoid them. Criticism began, adding to the feelings of many that the case should be left with the courts and she should go to jail. The research team encouraged people to keep meeting and talking.

Judge Davis, who was on the bench for this case, agreed to three court adjournments because people had not yet decided what to do, and MRM was not cooperating. Finally, MRM talked to the Chief and some of the elders again and agreed to talk to the community at a public meeting. The Chief placed total responsibility for organizing the meeting on MRM. Notices of the community meeting were posted, and people came to talk with her, and at her.

The Judge, getting weary of adjournments, eventually imposed the condition of no further adjournments. He also ordered DJP staff to attend any community meetings, count the people, list their names, keep minutes of the meeting, and report back to the court on what was decided, on who would take charge if probation were granted, and what the conditions of probation would be. This order placed the DJP in an awkward position that could have jeopardized our work in the community. It was not our role, nor our mandate, to force court requirements on the community. It was not our way of working either. We had always shared power with people and followed their instructions. Now that we had been placed in a position of following the court's instructions and, by virtue of the Judge's order, to report back on specific items, we felt we were forcing the court's criteria on the Dogrib process.

People met and discussed the options. One was to let the court decide, which meant at least a two- to four-year jail sentence for MRM, with probable release after she served one third of the time. Another court possibility was a suspended sentence and/or probation, since it was a first offence. Few people had confidence MRM would get probation unless the community really argued for it and the Lac La Martre Band Council was prepared to take some responsibility for supervision. There was considerable discussion as to what MRM should be asked to do if the community took responsibility. Also, they discussed who should be involved in her day-to-day supervision.

After considerable discussion, the community decided to support her request to stay in the community. Chief and Council agreed to provide her with community service work and to supervise her. A committee was set up to define the conditions of probation that would be recommended to the court. That committee consisted of Chief Isidore Zoe and four Band Councilors. A very knowledgeable elder, Alexis Flunkie from CAC, RCMP Constable Tom Roy, and Aggie Brockman (PD, DJP), were asked to assist the committee. MRM was also present at the meeting.

MRM was asked to accept the following conditions of probation for a period of two years:

1. a curfew from ten p.m. to six a.m.
2. restriction to the community except for medical reasons and/or compassionate ones, such as a funeral.
3. one day a week of community service supervised by the Band Council.

Restitution was discussed by the committee, but they decided not to set any amount to be repaid because that would be punishing family members. Gambling restrictions were also discussed but people felt a curfew was easier to enforce; they did not wish to set conditions that they themselves did not think they could enforce. In addition, the committee discussed asking the court not to have any criminal record in place for MRM. This request was never presented to the court.

The Chief and Council were to be responsible for supervision and for assigning the community service work. If MRM did not follow the rules, then any community member could report her to the Band Council or the RCMP. The RCMP could then charge her on a breach of probation and her case would return to the court. The DJP provided Judge Davis with the documentation of the community and committee meetings, as requested. The recommendation was to leave MRM in the community under the above terms of probation.

However, the court couldn't just accept the community recommendations. After debate between Counsels and further examination of MRM as to her ability to pay a fine, the Judge added a prohibition against any gambling and demanded that $5,000 compensation be paid by MRM. These two additions were in direct opposition to the committee's and elders' decisions; no opportunity was provided the elders or the Chief to speak against them.

Some community members, elders, and DJP staff felt these additions were unfair and that they also clearly undermined the authority of the community. Although there have been a few glitches and considerable community mumbling, MRM has honoured the conditions of her probation and, in fact, has given more than the required number of days for community service.[2] The payment of $5,000 has not been addressed. The only time MRM has been out of the community was to go to hospital for surgery.[3]

The process of reconciliation has continued, and while people watched MRM unremittingly in the beginning, people are more relaxed now. The conflict between younger people and the elders over the issue of jail, or no jail, was resolved by the imposition of the strict conditions of probation. As one woman put it, "I'd rather go to jail than not be allowed to play bingo or cards." Many youth thought jail would have been easier to accept than the public criticism, gossip, and watching. Some have begun to consider whether their own cases might be resolved in similar ways.

One young man, accused of breaking into and entering the Band Council office and being in possession of liquor, asked the Chief if the community could deal with his case. The Chief said "no" without consulting Council or elders. His explanation was that Council was not going to deal with any cases involving alcohol. That certainly limits the number of cases they will deal with since most offences include alcohol.

Summary

If we return to the section on the Dene process of dealing with problems, we see the elders and community followed their own traditional rules in dealing with MRM:

1. A complaint was made.
2. It was too serious for the Chief and Council to deal with alone.
3. The elders gathered and put MRM in the circle; she acknowledged her guilt.

---

2 One complaint was that MRM was seen walking around the streets of Yellowknife when she went to town for surgery. Another person reported MRM was gambling, and RCMP Constable Tom Roy went down and peeked through the window to see what was going on. He observed MRM sitting at the table drinking coffee alone while others were playing cards on the floor. Had the RCMP constable been acting officially on a complaint, it might have been wiser, and more courteous, for him to have knocked on the door and said so. Then the complaint could have been recorded and dismissed.

3 This was the case at the time of initial writing. During the March verification meetings, we were informed MRM had been allowed by the Chief to attend the New Year's dance where there was drinking, that she was spending five days a week in the office instead of one, thus not being at home with her children, that she was seen walking around at night, and, finally, that she had gone to Yellowknife with the Chief's permission to pick up her income tax cheque and to shop. She was allegedly seen at that time in the Gold Range bar. Some people complained to Crown Counsel, and he met with the RCMP to discuss breach charges. The Crown and RCMP decided not to charge MRM with breach of probation because she had had permission from the Chief to go to the dance and to town.

4. Harsh words were said and some demands were made.
5. Reconciliation began almost immediately.
6. MRM agreed to follow instructions and the matter was settled.
7. MRM did not follow the demands made on her so more gatherings took place and more harsh words were said. Although the traditional process was followed, there was some uncertainty about how to proceed when instructions were not followed. I think this was the result of the elders waiting for the Chief to do something and vice versa. The court's demand for precise conditions and identification of those responsible for making sure they were followed helped clarify roles and responsibilities.

In future cases, it would be useful to have the courts turn over the full power of decision-making to the community. For the court to agree to accept community conditions and then change them is not acceptable. Either the courts should proceed under their own rules and authority or they should turn the entire matter over to the community and they can decide whether they need RCMP assistance or court intervention. A combination of systems is not workable; this case shows clearly that the real power remained in the hands of the court rather than being transferred to the community, even when the court had agreed that the community could deal with the case.

The MRM case also shows that the community does not accept theft as appropriate behaviour, that the elders are prepared to provide guidance and harsh words, and that there are culturally appropriate ways of balancing things so reconciliation, restitution, and restoration of harmony is possible – even in modern times.

Case 2: The custody case

A young woman, Tina Bishop, pregnant with her second child, did not wish to marry the father of the child, Dolphus Apple. Tina's father, Narcisse Bishop, is raising her first child. During her pregnancy, Tina lived with her uncle Johnny Simpson and his non-Dene spouse Heather MacKenzie. During this time, people were talking to Tina about what she planned to do with the baby since she seemed not to want to keep it. A few relatives asked to adopt the baby. No decision was made before the birth.

When the baby girl, Sharlene, was born, Tina decided to keep her and returned to live with Johnny Simpson and Heather MacKenzie. The care of the baby was primarily left in their hands, and soon they were telling people they were "raising the child for Tina," that is following the rules for custom adoption. However, the father wanted the baby to be raised by his parents in his community of Rae Lakes, if Tina did not wish to keep her.

Shortly after her return from hospital in Yellowknife, Tina decided she did not want to keep the baby and told Dolphus he could come to Lac La Martre to get Sharlene. He took her back to Rae Lakes to his parents' home. When the baby was about two months old, Dolphus' parents asked the social worker, Gertie Brown, for custom adoption forms.[4] They wished to adopt and raise the baby. Gertie's interpreter was Johnny Simpson. Word arrived in Lac La Martre that the Apples wanted to keep the baby. Tina did not want the Apples to adopt Sharlene so her father, Narcisse, went to Rae Lakes to bring Sharlene back. Meanwhile, a few relatives in the community again asked if they could adopt her. However, Heather and Johnny wished to keep the baby, and she was left in their home, where Tina still lived while doing her up-grading in adult education.

Dolphus was advised by the social worker that if he wanted the baby, he would have to get a lawyer and go to court since Tina did not wish him to take the baby because Johnny and Heather were going to raise Sharlene for her. Dolphus then began a custody action against Tina.

By the time the Supreme Court arrived in Lac La Martre to hear the case, Tina's extended family had decided Sharlene should stay with Johnny and Heather or be raised by her grandfather, Narcisse, who was raising Tina's other child. Tina had indicated to her family that she wished to continue to have some involvement with the baby and that she wished Sharlene to stay where she was. Tina's plans were to go to high school in Rae-Edzo.

The arrival of the Supreme Court in Lac La Martre aroused considerable anger for several reasons, some of which were unrelated to the case. Judge Noonan was sitting and declared the hearings closed, as is the practice with custody cases. Members of the community did not understand this to be normal procedure and some were offended by not being able to attend.

The counsel for Tina had asked the RCMP to serve subpoenas on nineteen witnesses in Lac La Martre and another nine in Rae Lakes. Those in Lac La Martre were served but the Rae Lakes ones were not. Therefore, a major problem arose, which made people very angry. An elder had died in Rae-Edzo, and it is expected that elders and relatives from other communities will attend funerals. The Rae Lakes elders were able

---

4 These are legal forms provided by Social Services. Custom adoption is recognized under the NWT Ordinances.

to go to the funeral but the Lac La Martre elders apparently thought they would be arrested if they got on the charter because they had to appear in court as witnesses. They stayed. The RCMP officer denied telling people he would arrest elders if they got on the plane. However, several elders said they understood him to say they could not board the charter because they had been subpoenaed, and one of the DJP researchers reported the term "arrest" was used.

The Lac La Martre elders were very upset, because they missed the funeral and, secondly, because they were never called to testify.[5] However, what angered them most of all was that the court had come in to deal with a custody case that the extended family considered to be already settled.

Judge Noonan responded positively to Chief Zoe's request that the court not meet until the Lac La Martre elders had a chance to meet with the young people involved. She adjourned for several hours. The community meeting was carried out almost totally in the Dogrib language, and the DJP staff summarized comments for me from time to time. The Apple family had no elders with them and felt quite threatened by the circle process. The elders from Lac La Martre chastised them for claiming a female child. Female children are considered to be the property of the mother and her extended family. The elders expressed their concern for the child because people were "fighting" over her, and she might come to some harm. The Chief informed the Apples that the community had already decided the baby would stay where she was. The Apples countered with an attack on Johnny Simpson saying he had "thrown away" his own children from his previous marriage and was with a non-Dene woman whom they did not wish to raise their grandchild.

Some of the Lac La Martre elders agreed with this and also gave Johnny "harsh words." Johnny's response was that he was over his alcohol problems and now had a different life. Several elders indicated they had "warned" Johnny about living with a non-Dene woman, and several said they did not wish her to raise the baby.

The Apples said this circle process was not the way things got settled in Rae Lakes and they were going to continue with the court case. They wanted to raise Sharlene since her mother did not want to care for her. The paternal

---

5   It seemed unfortunate that only three Lac La Martre witnesses were called: Heather MacKenzie and Gertie Brown, who were non-Dene and Johnny Simpson, who testified on Tina's behalf. Only Dolphus' father Alphonse testified on his son's behalf.

grandfather also made a reference to the father's constitutional right to have his child, especially since the mother did not wish to raise her.

The young people, Tina and Dolphus, were asked by the Chief if they had anything to say. Dolphus, referring to comments made about his responsibility to marry Tina since he admitted impregnating her, said he would gladly marry Tina. Tina responded that she would not marry him. The meeting ended with no consensus achieved.

The court reconvened. Chief Zoe had asked that I be permitted to observe the proceedings on behalf of the Band and the Dene Justice Project. Both Counsels and their clients agreed and the Judge allowed me in, provided I kept all proceedings confidential.

The court resumed in the morning, and the judge was informed earlier by the Chief that the elders had met through the night and that the two sets of grandparents had met separately to talk with each other. She adjourned again, asking the grandparents and Sharlene's parents to meet with her. While the judge was meeting, the Counsels were talking with their clients' extended families, the social worker, and others.

The judge's session with the grandparents did not result in an agreement and the court resumed in the afternoon. Some witnesses waited to appear. Prior to the start of court, Tina's Counsel asked the judge if I could appear as an expert witness. I had earlier declined to do so since the elders were all available, and they had the expert information that she needed. The judge declined to have me appear.

During the afternoon, the elders continued meeting among themselves with members of the extended family and the young people. They sent a message to the judge that they thought they had some suggestions. Court was adjourned again so the Counsels could meet with the families and elders. It opened again for a short evening session and reached agreement that both Counsels would bring community recommendations to the court the next morning.

In the morning, the court was told that the Lac La Martre elders and the Apples had come to an agreement. The judge made their agreement the basis of her written decision.[6] Baby Sharlene would remain in the custody of her mother, Tina, and was to move to her grandfather's (Narcisse's) home, with or without Tina, within a month. Dolphus was to provide country food and/or cash for the baby's diapers, milk, etc. on a regular basis. Dolphus could visit his daughter on forty-eight hours

---

6 I am free to say what these decisions were since the final order was sent to me by the Court Clerk and is in the public domain.

notice to Narcisse and Tina. He could take her to Rae Lakes one week in each six-month period. This decision would be reviewed within the year.

Most people in Lac La Martre seemed satisfied with the decision. However, the baby did not move to Narcisse's house but remained with Johnny and Heather. Tina left to go to school in Rae-Edzo. Dolphus filed for sole custody of the child because she was not being cared for by either her mother or her grandfather but by third parties. And so it all began again.

By this time, the baby had bonded to Heather and Johnny, who also had adopted a newborn boy from Rae-Edzo. Tina is alleged to have told Dolphus he could have Sharlene because she was in school and would not raise the child. Dolphus then sent word to Lac La Martre that he was coming to get the baby. Heather and Johnny contacted a lawyer and the RCMP told Dolphus to stay out of Lac La Martre until he had a court order in his hand saying he could take Sharlene.[7] Dolphus did not come to Lac La Martre and Heather and Johnny then joined in the custody action against him.

This new action reactivated the case and created a round of written affidavits on behalf of Tina. Affidavits were filed by Johnny, Heather, Tina, and Marie Adele Rabesca (Tina's aunt and DJP staff member), in the cause of the baby staying where she was. The Chief also sent a letter to the judge, suggesting in no uncertain terms that the baby be left where she was and that the decision of Tina's extended family and Lac La Martre elders be respected.

Marie Adele's affidavit was very long and not too accurate. Counsel for the defendant Tina had written it and faxed it to her. MAR did not read it in full, and it was not gone over with her by Counsel or the RCMP officer when he notarized it. She advised Counsel, by phone, that some facts were not correct. For example, it stated she was an elder, which she is not. Counsel told MAR it was too late to change anything and asked her to sign it and get it notarized. The DJP team received a copy, and we asked MAR what she planned to do to correct the contents. We were concerned about her being held in contempt, if she were called to testify and if she were cross-examined. Marie Adele then asked the CAC elders for advice, and they told her to change it so it would be accurate. Aggie and I were asked

---

7 The DJP staff was not clear on what authority the RCMP did this since Dolphus had, at the very least, court consent to see the baby. Constable Roy explained to me that he had told Dolphus not to come because he knew there would be big trouble if Dolphus tried to take the baby away from Johnny and Heather, which was likely the case. The question still remains: on what legal basis did the RCMP forbid Dolphus to come to Lac La Martre?

to help rewrite it. A new affidavit was filed. The affidavits of the others also included some inaccurate statements, but they were not changed.

The court met twice on the case and adjourned. Tina's Counsel withdrew from the case. The baby stayed with Johnny and Heather.

Shortly after New Year's Day, 1992, people reported there was much drinking in town, including parties at Heather and Johnny's. A fight broke out and Heather and the children found themselves out in the snow. Shortly after, Heather realized their baby boy seemed ill. When the nurses could not find anything wrong with him, Heather took him to the Yellowknife hospital where he was examined and found to have a broken leg and two broken fingers. The doctor called Social Services, who took the baby into custody. Heather returned to Lac La Martre alone.

People then became worried about Sharlene's safety. The elders met again. Tina was called, but no one called Dolphus. There was concern that Sharlene might also have been injured; she was checked out by the nurses and was well. The DJP team got involved in discussions about the baby because of her relationship to Marie Adele and because everyone thought "something" should be done. Aggie and I pointed out that the family was already breaking the court order since Sharlene had been meant to go live with Narcisse more than six months before. The Chief and elders decided that Sharlene should go to Narcisse. Tina and Narcisse agreed; Johnny and Heather refused. There was no court order to remove Sharlene. The RCMP and Social Service investigation on the little boy's injuries was very slow to start, and no charges were ever laid. Sharlene remained with Johnny and Heather; their baby boy was placed with his relatives in Rae-Edzo. Meanwhile, Dolphus continued to pursue custody and another court hearing was scheduled for July. In July, Dolphus Apple did not appear. Johnny and Heather received custody of Sharlene.

Summary

If we turn to Dene traditional ways of dealing with things as outlined in the section on family, we see that there were several traditions called into play in this case:

1. The circle process to deal with issues between families was put in place. It did not result in consensus because the Rae Lakes family decided to stay with the non-Dene court.
2. There was consensus among the Lac La Martre elders that female babies belong to the mother and should be raised by her or her close relatives.

3. Relatives on both sides were available and wanted to adopt the baby.

4. The baby was adopted by her great uncle and his non-Dene spouse. Elders do not appear to be totally satisfied with this arrangement due to the history of alcohol abuse by both people, the fact the man already has a family he does not support and because he has a history of physical violence and past convictions for assault. Some people said they did not want a non-Dene woman raising Dene babies.

5. People agreed the mother's father should have the baby.

6. People wanted the matter settled because they feared that some harm would come to the baby if adults continued to fight over her.

7. People felt the court should not have intervened in this matter since the care of children is a Dogrib responsibility and one which they are willing to accept even if reaching a resolution is difficult.

If we analyze the conflict between the families, we see the court intervention has far- reaching implications. Had the court not come, it is likely elders from both communities would have sat together after the funeral. The court timing was poor because of the funeral, which no one could have anticipated. The fact that some of the subpoenas were served and others were not meant some elders were prevented from going to a funeral, which made them feel badly and made them angry.

The conflict that arose between the two families was not so much one of disagreement about where the baby should stay but focused on the issue of how the decision should be made and by whom. The Rae Lakes people objected to their elders not being a part of the discussions, while the Lac La Martre people felt the decision should be theirs alone, based on the tradition of keeping female babies in their mothers' communities.

There was also some miscommunication between the court and the elders, possibly because information was filtered through a poor interpreter when the judge met with the grandparents and parents of the child, or because the elders' decisions were presented by lawyers not very familiar with local customs.

None of the non-Dene lawyers and the court officers seemed to understand that giving custody to the baby's maternal grandfather meant he had to care for the child himself. Indeed, it doesn't make much sense to give an older man the charge of a baby when he has neither a wife nor an older female in the house willing to care for a child. People hoped the mother would be helped by relatives to care for her baby by leaving her where she was. The grandfather, as head of the extended family, would be the senior person responsible for making sure the child was cared for and raised well.

This misunderstanding led to further complications: 1) The mother and grandfather (and community) are in breach of a court order; 2) the father renewed his fight for custody of his daughter.

It is the interaction of the Dogrib and non-Dene systems that is the problem, not either system in itself. It is impossible to mix the systems and keep things uncomplicated and straightforward. If the Lac La Martre Dogrib elders had been left to their own decisions, they would have made sure the child was left with a relative and well-cared for. The mother would have been responsible for the child, but this responsibility would have been shared by her female relatives and the senior male head of the family, Narcisse.

Case 3: The marten pelts disappear

This case is included because it is an example of how Dogrib rules can work very well on their own.

The school gym is open to the community in the late afternoons and evenings. A group of young men play basketball regularly. One night they arrived to find themselves locked out.

·Following the theft of two tanned marten pelts, which hung on the gym wall, the Community Education Committee (CEC) decided to resolve the issue using Dogrib rules. They closed the gym to all users, including the regular school classes, until the marten pelts were returned or replaced with ones of equal value.

The gym remained closed for more than two weeks, and then the young men got annoyed because they could not play their game. They knew who had stolen the martens, met at his house, and told him he had to give them back. He admitted he sold them for a good price. The group made a decision: they would collect enough money to buy other martens and the thief would not be allowed to come to the gym, or participate in any other activity with them, until he had paid them back for the new marten pelts. One of the men bought two marten pelts and was allowed into the gym to hang them up. The elders' wisdom was that the martens were not of the same value, but the CEC was prepared to accept them anyway. The young men went back to playing basketball; the school children got back to classes. The matter had been closed.

No charges were laid by the RCMP because Constable Les Dell accepted that the local people would take responsibility for settling the matter. No one wanted charges laid; the CEC wanted to try their hand at the Dogrib ways of dealing with things. It worked.

Summary:

This situation follows the Dogrib tradition:

1. A complaint arose.
2. The CEC was prepared to deal with it.
3. An offence affected the collectivity; no one got to use the gym.
4. The offender was confronted by his peers – the ones most affected.
5. He acknowledged his offence and said he would make restitution.
6. He did not have all the money to buy the furs back so his peers helped him out. Reconciliation began.
7. The gym reopened; the offender was not allowed in (shunned) until he repaid the full amount.
8. Harmony was restored between the basketball group and the CEC. The matter was closed. There was no court record of the theft.

7

Conflicts between Dogrib and Non-Dene Justice Systems

This chapter is a result of various discussions of data and cases. These discussions took place between project staff, various counsels, court officers, the Band Council and elders, and Technical Advisory Committee (TAC) members.

Has the research proved the existence of traditional rules?

The information provided by the elders about how things worked in the past and how people maintained order and restored it when it was out of balance indicates clearly that there was a set of rules that had to be followed and were enforceable. In serious cases, offences were dealt with by the adult community members; less serious ones were handled by the *k'àowos*.

It would be impossible to imagine the survival of a human society without the existence of rules to make it function. The Dogrib people have survived; the environment, people, spirits, and animals are still here. What is not present is stability of behaviour in the human population. Therefore, the balance among human, animal, and natural worlds is not in place currently. Questions that arose in many discussions follow.

Do Dogrib rules fit the non-Dene concept of law or are they considered to be "traditions" or "customs"?

Non-Dene criteria should not be applied to Dogrib "rules for doing things the right way." If one were to assign a rank order to Dogrib rules, traditions, and customs, it would look much the same as non-Dene laws, traditions, and customs. Rules and laws would come first, as they are critical to the maintenance of the society; traditions and customs would follow. If one looks at how non-Dene laws are made, taught, and enforced and how they have evolved, we see a very similar process to that in place for Dogrib rules.

Our laws are made by Parliament, passed by majority vote, tested in the courts, and then applied to all citizens. The rules for appropriate behaviour are taught by parents, teachers, lawyers, police, and other functionaries. They are passed down from generation to generation in writing and orally. They change over time, adapting to changes in society. They cover a broad range of behaviours and possible misbehaviours.

When laws are breached, there are established ways of dealing with the offender. These ways vary from mild reprimands, official warnings and police charges. More serious charges are dealt with in court by one judge, or by the judge and a jury, or by a number of judges.

The offender has the option of pleading guilty or not guilty. If judged to be guilty, the person is punished by a fine or loss of freedom, or is required to do community service, or is let go to live "properly," that is, given a "chance." Punishment is meant to deter further offences. The individual can appeal the court's decision and may get a different decision at a higher court.

If we look at the Dogrib system in the same way, we see that rules were made by the elders in the tribal region at annual gatherings. The decisions were made by consensus, however, not by majority vote. This implies a greater uniformity and, therefore, a greater strength in making sure the rules are known and followed. Consensus cannot be challenged so there is no test of the rules. They were, however, applied to all Dogrib people in the region, probably more uniformly than non-Dene laws are applied. The rules were passed down from generation to generation through the oral teachings of elders and through the example of their own behaviours. Rules were also taught by parents and medicine people. They also were adapted over time to meet the needs of a changing society.

When rules were breached, there were established ways of dealing with the offender. These ways varied from mild ridicule to harsh words and warnings, or being placed in the circle. The offender was dealt with by one person, the *k'àowo*, if the offence was minor; he or she was dealt with by the *yabahti* and all the senior people in the group if it was a very serious breach.

This is virtually the same process as coming before a judge and jury, the difference being that the jury is not a group of peers for the offender, but a group of senior men and women.

The Dogrib offender does not have the option of pleading "not guilty." There is no such concept in their ways of doing things. However, no action is taken against an individual unless people are sure that something wrong has been done by the individual which affects the safety and well-being of the collective.

Once the decision is made, the offender is not punished. Rather, the group demands that he or she face the victim, that restitution be made, that reconciliation start. These processes restore social, political, and spiritual harmony, a process not included in the non-Dene system. If the offender does not do as bid in serious matters, then he or she has to leave the group. There can be no appeal to any higher authority since the *yabahti* and elders are the highest authorities in Dene society.[1]

It seems we can argue that the processes are very similar. A few objections that have been made by non-Dene are discussed below:

1. Traditional Dogrib rules are not written down, while non-Dene laws are.

There doesn't seem to be a valid reason for rejecting Dogrib rules because they were not written down. They were passed down orally and were potentially as effective as anything that might have been written down. Perhaps they were even more effective because they were built on consensus and were well understood by all members of the society.

The need to write things down currently appears to be important to the Dene, thus the importance of documenting traditional environmental knowledge, justice, governance, and oral history. The justice rules could be updated now, decided by consensus, and written down in Dogrib and English. They need not be as complicated as non-Dene laws. Many

---

1 The lack of a "not guilty" plea and the lack of an appeal system may be viewed by some as non-democratic in this day and age. One might also argue that the size of the society determines whether the Dene system might work. The team agrees that the size of the group must be small enough for people to "know" who did the wrongful act. Most Dene communities are this size; the exceptions are the multicultural centres such as Yellowknife, Inuvik, Ft. Smith, and Hay River. Victim compensation is relatively new in the non-Dene system, as is the recent trend to have those found guilty of certain crimes, such as rape, face their victims.

Canadian statutes and codes could be eliminated from a Dogrib system in the interests of efficient delivery of justice in small communities.

2.   Dogrib rules do not have the force of non-Dene laws.

Why not? They certainly seem to have worked in the past to keep the society functioning in a smooth way. Offenders were often harshly dealt with (such as in the case of banishment) and life went on. They were forceful enough that the Dogribs have survived as a distinct group who still maintain their language, culture, and many traditions including justice ones.

3.   Traditional Dogrib rules cannot deal with today's offences.

Of course not! Nor could non-Dene laws made in the 1900s deal with the complex behaviors of the 1990s. All societies have to update laws on a continuing basis. The evolution of Dogrib rules has fallen behind because of settlement, increase in populations, loss of elders' instructional roles and the imposition of the non-Dene legal system. However, if elders and others wanted to do so, they could meet and come to a consensus on how to deal with most unacceptable behaviour in their communities. There are some indications that many people do not feel confident about dealing with murder, rape and incest yet.

4.   Traditional Dogrib rules are in conflict with the Canadian Charter of Rights and Freedoms.

Perhaps they are. The issue of the application of the Charter is one with which the Royal Commission on Aboriginal Affairs is now wrestling. As well, the Assembly of First Nations (AFN) is looking at how the Charter might be by-passed in the move to self-determination. The Native Council of Canada and various aboriginal women's groups are looking at ways to prevent the AFN override. Obviously this matter is not going to be resolved easily.

It would be an interesting process to develop a Dene Charter of Rights, which could be the basis for the development of new Dene rules. If regional consensus could be reached on such a contemporary Dogrib Charter, perhaps the Canadian Charter should not apply. As long as all human rights are protected, what would the issue be? Innovative ways of dealing with human rights and legal issues can be pursued by the Dogrib people themselves in an attempt to come to grips with self-government and the establishment of a Dogrib justice system. Obviously, this cannot be done quickly or easily.

5. *Can there be a system of justice without the concept of "not guilty"?*

If the Dogrib system is going to operate by consensus, then one can assume that the offender's case will be dealt with by people who know exactly what happened in their own communities. It might mean some minor offences would fall through the net, but all major ones would be dealt with because the group would have the information in hand. Since the overriding goal is to maintain harmony within the small collective, any wrongful accusations would not go unchallenged.

6. *If there is no punishment, what will stop the individual from committing the same offence again?*

The non-Dene system has not been particularly successful in stopping individuals from repeating or escalating crimes. The Dogrib system would have this ability, at least in small communities, because of the shame, the involvement of relatives and all community members in the judgment, the enforcement of mechanisms to restore harmony and balance, and because of the embarrassment of the public decision-making process. Needless to say, some individuals would repeat offences, but probably not many would. Repeat offenders could be sent to island camps to come to grips with themselves through sobriety and under the supervision and teaching of elders.

7. *Traditional ways of teaching the rules and dealing with those who break them are too harsh on women and children; they would not be considered acceptable today.*

In the past, non-Dene ways were also very harsh, especially with regard to the disciplining of women and children. Today, there are few women anywhere who are willing to be treated abusively (emotionally or physically) by men. Any new Dogrib rules would have to deal even-handedly with men, women, and youth. The line between discipline and abuse needs to be clearly defined.[2]

---

2 Non-Dene courts have not protected women from abuse with any consistency. One-day sentences for men who have sexually abused women have been prevalent recently, including a case in Lac La Martre. The 1992 Sanderson case raised the issues very clearly. The message from women that the abuse must end seems to have by-passed a lot of men, including judges. The Dogrib people are no further behind in this than the non-Dene.

Mary Madelaine Nitsiza.

Johnny Bishop and the late Menton Mantla waiting for a plane to leave.
Nick Mantla (son) is standing in the background.

8. Dogrib rules would not be as complex nor as technically excellent as non-Dene ones.

Do they have to be? Non-Dene laws are not understood by, or even familiar to, most Canadians. In general, most citizens understand the basic laws that keep traffic running, streets safe, property protected, etc. Dogrib rules would deal with similar day-to-day social control. This could be an exciting opportunity to make the rules understood and agreed to by all Dene.

Reconciliation and restitution are humane, direct, and fairly effective ways of dealing with unacceptable behaviour. Values differ between cultural groups and these differences need to be reflected in local rules and in their applications.

Likely, there would be some areas of law that might have to overlap in the two systems initially. In part, this will have to be decided by the group taking back responsibility for justice. For example, what would happen to a non-Dene transient, or a resident, who commits an offence in a Dene community? One would hope that Dene rules would be applicable to all persons in their jurisdiction within their traditional territories, although some different means of dealing with people in urban centres might have to be evolved. Many negotiations will have to take place on matters considered to be within the Canadian Criminal Code because an alternate system might be able to deal with its own citizens but not those from elsewhere.

Conflicts between systems

The above section has dealt with anticipated and stated arguments of some non-Dene and Dene against the establishment of a separate Dogrib system of justice. Let us now turn to a consideration of actual conflicts between the two systems which have been reported and observed during the course of the project.

How do the Lac La Martre people perceive the non-Dene Court and its officers? What are the general complaints?

1. The Lac La Martre people indicated in various interviews and discussions that they do not like being "judged" by non-Dene. They do not feel that the officers of the court are knowledgeable about the Dogrib culture and their feelings and values.

2. They do not like having English as the sole language of the court. People complain that interpreters picked out of the community at random

when the court arrives are not trained and often misinterpret because of their own views and involvement with the accused.[3]

Interpretation provided by those who have taken the legal interpreter's course, but have little experience, is also criticized as being inaccurate. On one occasion, the legal interpreter was so shy and so lacking in confidence, no one could hear her; the Chief and native court worker took over translation. Sometimes there are earphones; sometimes not. When there are not, the physical setting of the court often prohibits elders from hearing the translation unless they are allowed to move closer and the officers of the court position their tables to face the observers. Simultaneous translation, when provided, is extremely difficult for elders and some others to follow. Consecutive interpretation is clearer and allows people to follow more readily.

3. They are intimidated by the court setting and its rituals. People do not understand why the court officers wear gowns or what the swearing-in ritual means. They do not understand the legal language.

4. They do not understand why crimes against property sometimes bring more serious legal penalties than crimes against persons.

5. They do not understand why some laws that seem irrelevant are enforced. For example, they do not understand why people who do not drive on the winter road are charged with driving without a licence and/ or without insurance when they only drive the few miles of road in Lac La Martre. Since several people have been arrested for failure to pay fines for this offence and have served time because they could not pay, people are resentful. Other offences that they consider to be more serious, such as assault, sometimes only receive one-day sentences and minimum fines.[4]

---

3   In 1992, Johnny Simpson interpreted for the pretrial of Francis Zoe, who was alleged to have sexually assaulted his step-daughter. People complained for days after the court session that he had not done a "straight" translation, that he had left things out and added others, and that he gave a lengthy statement of his own opinion. Similarly, I suspect the confusion in the Supreme Court Apples-Bishop custody case arose because of the translation provided at one point when the judge, counsels, and families met.

4   There is also a matter of discretionary power on the part of the RCMP. When Constable Les Dell was in the community, he did not charge people who drove only in the community with vehicle-operation offences. He kept at them to get their licences and insurance but did not charge them if they had no money to do so. Constable Tom Roy has taken a much more rigid enforcement position on this and other matters, and so more people are being charged. It should be noted that getting the licences and insurance adds roundtrip airfare to the cost since Yellowknife officials and insurance companies will not send them by mail.

6. They resent what they perceive to be "interference" by the courts in matters they have usually decided on their own. The Apple-Bishop case is a good example of this. The reasoning is based on the Dogrib rules that children are considered the property of women and their extended families. The elders feel families should be left to decide family matters.

7. They object to the removal of young adults from the community for minor crimes, especially for non-payment of fines. They do not feel that being poor is a justifiable reason to put people in jail. Some people said this is a way for non-Dene to "make money" from the problems of the Dogribs at Lac La Martre. In general, Lac La Martre people are opposed to any youth going to jail; they feel they should be dealt with in the community. As well, people seem to feel the only reason people should be jailed is for major violent crimes such as rape, sexual assault, and murder.[5]

8. They object to the little time the court officers spend in the community. The plane flies in, the legal-aid lawyer and native court worker (if present) take a few minutes with clients, aware of the remaining court officials waiting for them. Since the Dogrib way of dealing with problems is to talk at length about things over a long period of time (e.g., the Mary Rose Moosenose case) in order to come to a consensus, the non-Dene way of doing things so quickly is offensive. The Lac La Martre people feel this shows a lack of respect for community members and traditions and that matters are not dealt with properly in a way that people can understand what is going on.

In general, people feel discussions should take place in the Dogrib language, that cases should be explained so that people know what is happening and that the Chief and others should be permitted to speak to the court in their own language about their concerns in each case. People feel too many charges are made on matters that could be talked through and resolved locally, if charges were not laid. Many feel the issues and problems could be dealt with in more culturally appropriate ways. Their preference would be to control their own system and to deal with most matters now, with the exception of the major crimes mentioned, without court or RCMP intervention.

---

5 During the life of the project, and more recently during the verification meetings, elders talked at length about young people committing suicide because they were jailed for minor crimes, e.g., non-payment of fines. Since there have been no young Dogribs who have committed suicide in jail, or indeed in Lac La Martre, the research team is puzzled by the depth of feeling and persistence of these statements.

Lac La Martre people welcomed the early arrival of the Crown Prosecutor on several occasions when he came in to the community the day before court was held. They appreciated his consultations with people on the Mary Rose Moosenose case and his general interest in the community. Most of all, they appreciated having the same prosecutor for each court session. As well, they appreciated having Judge Davis there regularly and noted his respect for the elders by having them sit close to the interpreter and for organizing the court physically so they could see and hear.

We turn now to the conclusions and recommendations proposed by the CAC, the research team, and the community members of Lac La Martre.

Conclusions and Recommendations

Conclusions

The DJP research team never doubted that the Dogrib people had rules and that they worked well for traditional times. The overlay of the non-Dene legal system removed responsibility from the Dogrib for dealing with social problems in their own society. Many other areas of responsibility were also removed from the Dogrib. They lost control over the education of their children, over language and culture, and over their spiritual lives. Now they know that if they are to survive as First Nations, they must reclaim their knowledge, abilities, beliefs, and lives.

The process of "taking back" responsibility will not be an easy one nor will it be done quickly. At the time of contact, the Dene were a strong group of people with their own institutions and cultural systems; they had governments, leadership, religion, social networks, and trade routes, and they held their hunting/trapping lands in common. They balanced their human, spiritual, and natural worlds with integrity, and an effective stewardship maintained their natural resources. These highly developed and self-determining nations became undeveloped through contact. Like all situations of colonialism, people became dependent on the non-Dene institutions, and, as a result, their own began to lose strength and meaning.

The overall effect of colonization has been primarily negative for the Dene. While some parts of their physical life have become better, other things have become so bad they are no longer tolerable. In order to survive as people, the Dene now have no choice but to return to their own traditions and to reclaim their institutions. Some will be irrelevant for modern times, and some will have been forgotten.

Nevertheless, if the basic traditional values can be reinstated, the forms of modern Dene institutions can be whatever they become – a mix of old and new technologies, ideas, and concepts. What is important is the process by which they are put in place and maintained. What is at stake are the lives and cultures of generations to come. Compromises are not enough nor are adaptations of non-Dene systems where power remains with the non-Dene. The ability to survive with confidence and a better quality of life depend basically on the willingness of people to take back responsibility for their own lives and then to rebuild Dene values and institutions so that balance is restored between the natural, spirit, and human worlds once again.

This cannot be done all at once. The recommendations suggest where to start and what phases should follow each other. Obviously, people need to start with issues on which they can reach consensus now. The process may also require some facilitation from external resource people, both Dene and non-Dene. In some instances, joint ventures between Dogrib people and non-Dene may be the fastest route by which they can reclaim self-determination.

Non-Dene may not be enthusiastic about a process that will require them to give back power, authority, and funds so Dene can do their own thing. One argument will be that Canadian laws are good laws and that they have been in effect and tested over a long period of time. Therefore, they should apply to all Canadians and a segment of the population cannot be "allowed" to make their own laws – or choose not to follow Canadian ones.

It is up to the Dene to determine if, in fact, they consider themselves to be Canadians or if they are sovereign nations in themselves. The fact that Dene rules have not been written down does not mean that they do not exist and that they have not been tested. In fact, the research done in the community shows quite clearly that Dogrib rules did exist, were tested, did work and are still known to many people.

Because many non-Dene do not understand, or even know, what the Dene rules are and how they work is not a reason to insist that only non-Dene laws can be used to handle Dene social problems. Canadians have, over time, changed and rejected the British and French laws which were the beginning of Canadian laws. In Quebec, Canadian criminal laws apply, but Napoleonic civil laws continue to be used. It might be that the Dene could continue to use Canadian criminal laws but recreate their own civil laws.

Others will argue that Dogrib rules cannot deal with the major crimes now handled by non-Dene courts. They will say the concepts of justice that underlie such laws are missing in Dogrib thought. The research showed, however, that the belief systems and the rules that flowed from them are very much present in Dogrib rules. We suggest that most of these concepts are very usable in current Canadian law.

Take, for example, the literal translation of *"dǫ hǫłį gha wekèe natsèdla"* [rape], the "tearing apart of a person" that is, the woman's clothes are torn, her body is torn and her soul is torn. If the non-Dene system used that definition, convictions, sentences, and compensation in the non-Dene courts would likely be greater than they now are. As well, this Dogrib definition of rape is clearly adequate for dealing with violence against Dogrib women.

There are those who will say that old ways cannot work in modern times so the Dogrib traditional rules are not appropriate for current times. The data suggest differently. Indeed, in the case of Mary Rose Moosenose, traditional ways involving consensus, admission of guilt, reconciliation, restitution, and restoration of harmony have all worked very well.

Others may say the resource laws are not scientific and therefore not valid for resource management. However, our research findings, and those of Johnson and Ruttan in the Ft. Good Hope Traditional Environmental Knowledge Project, show that the Dene "understand many of the complex ecological linkages ... habitat use, etc. and ... this knowledge combines both personal experience and the teaching of elders passed down from generation to generation over countless years."[1] Further, the Dene rules for resource management that the Ft. Good Hope project identified are identical to the Lac La Martre ones, which indicates the rules in Denendeh may be relatively uniform and thus applicable to all Dene.

Some people may argue the strong spiritual component of Dene rules has no realistic base in general law. However, British common laws were based on strong moral principles and were no less "spiritual" than Dene traditional rules, except to the extent to which people recall and use

---

1   M. Johnson and Robert Ruttan. *Traditional Dene Environmental Knowledge.* Hay River, NWT: Dene Cultural Institute, 1992.

APRIL NITSIZA

Aggie Brockman and Bernice Beaverho.

Sign outside house/office, made by Archie Beaverho.

these beliefs. Recall that in the family unit, we identified values that were almost identical to those of Roman Catholicism, making it very easy for missionaries to gain acceptance because there was so little conflict between the sets of beliefs. Further, spiritual beliefs do not take away from the personal experience and scientific knowledge of the elders. To the extent that Canon law and Common law reflect the values of European societies, Dene rules reflect the same values for their societies.

Finally, some people may be sceptical about the ability of the Dogrib to run their own legal affairs. The chapter on political rules indicates clearly that, given proper leadership, things can work well. A return to selection of leaders by consensus might solve some of the current problems described by elders with regard to chiefs "not having strong words." The case studies provided in chapter 6 indicate that when the Lac La Martre people sat together, they came up with ideas that judges had no difficulty accepting. One assumes this was because the solutions were very close to what the court might also have decided.

Did the research meet its own goals?

Yes! We set out to establish that the Dogrib had a system of rules to keep the community functioning in an orderly way. We have shown this is true in the areas of resource rules, family rules and political authority. We showed that the rules were passed down from generation to generation, that they were enforced, and that there were set ways of dealing with individuals who broke the rules.

We noted where the rules for women were more severe than ones for men and that some rules were in effect only for women.

We established that there was no concept in Dene rules of "not guilty" – a major difference between Dene rules and Canadian law.

We established that the Dene legal system was not punitive. Rather it was based on concepts of reconciliation, restitution, and the restoration of harmony – all concepts lacking force in the non-Dene legal system.

We also determined that the Lac La Martre people want to take back responsibility for their own system of social control and indeed have started doing it. Finally, we noted that there is not consensus between old and young. The elders would prefer to remove themselves from the non-Dene system, while the young fear the traditional system would be harsher than the non-Dene one. Each group tends to stick with the system it knows best, and considerable work will have to be done to convince the younger people that the values that underlie the traditional system will ensure a more humane system for the future.

Recommendations

Recommendations are based on discussions with people in Lac La Martre about where they think things should change and how. Data and recomendations have been discussed and agreed upon by the Lac La Martre Community Advisory Committee, the elders of Lac La Martre, Rae Lakes, Snare Lakes, Rae-Edzo, Detah, and Ndilǫ. As well, public community meetings were held in the same communities. There were no significant differences of opinion between or among Lac La Martre and the other communities. We consider that this regional perspective and agreement makes the findings applicable to the whole region.

The recommendations approved by the Lac La Martre elders, CAC, and community are:

1. *Alcohol abuse must be tackled. The community recommended:*

    a) An alcohol treatment team should be brought into Lac La Martre for an extended period of time, at least three to six months. The team should be aboriginal, such as the staff from Northern Addictions or the group from Alkali Lake, B.C. or staff from Nechi Institute, Alberta. The program should not only help people to give up alcohol abuse, it should also provide some training for people who want to run support groups.[2]

    b) A series of healing circles should be established: one for women, one for men, one for girls, and one for boys. Once some healing has taken place within these groups, the adults need to meet with each other and then with the youths to deal with the hurt of past abuse and neglect. New ways of dealing with anger and frustration need to be learned. Men who disclose previous abuse of children or adult women should be dealt with by the Dogrib Circle, composed of adult members of the community. The goal would be to heal these men, not to punish them. They could be isolated on one of the islands and visited regularly by the elders in order to learn how to behave properly again. If victims desired restitution or reconciliation, these processes could be put in place.

    c) The alcohol program set out in the new health curriculum in the NWT schools should be taught. Many teachers do not give it time or treat it seriously. Perhaps a community health teacher or health nurse needs to take on this responsibility. It could be taught in Dogrib. Such alcohol and drug education should be accompanied by a training

---

2 If there were as many cases of measles as there are cases of alcohol addiction, there would be a major health team in the community to help out. Why is the same approach not available to people who are equally sick from alcohol?

program for young children that teaches them that they can say "no" and that they can take some control of their own lives and that they are competent and worthy.

It will take many years to eliminate the use of alcohol in Lac La Martre. In the short run, it will take some convincing to get many people involved in treatment. However, people should remember that, in Alkali Lake, the Shuswap people had three sober adults at the end of year one. Ten years later, only two people drank.

2. *A community education program needs to take place before a pilot project begins and before a Dogrib justice committee is selected.*

During the course of this project, the community has been involved in several ways: Adults have visited and sat in on meetings; children have visited, but are not quite sure what we were doing. Elders have been extensively involved, and the leadership is aware of what we were doing, and why. Young adults, many of whom don't know their own history and traditional culture, have been the most absent group. They are most ambivalent about reestablishing any traditional ways that they perceive to be much harsher than non-Dene ones.

It is important that this group be involved in any new ways of handling problems in the community. They probably represent the group in the courts most often, mainly on minor issues, but sometimes on more serious thefts and assaults. This group needs time to learn their traditions and to reconnect with elders.

The community justice education program should focus on discussion of the report and its recommendations with the goal of reaching consensus on new directions. The program should also enable youth, young adults, and others to connect with the elders in order to rebuild respect.

Elders could be invited into the school on a regular basis to teach young children their heritage. They could accompany children and youth out on the land on trips designed to teach bush skills, competence, sharing, and self-reliance, as well as to expand their knowledge and identity. The spiritual component of being on the land should be emphasized by parents and elders.

The use of the Dogrib language in the school and on the land would improve the spoken language; Dogrib literacy would not only provide a basis for pride but would allow young Dogrib people to listen to, and to read, their elders' stories.

An elder-youth group could pair individuals in ways that would allow respect and knowledge to grow and perhaps return people to caring and sharing. Values outlined in the section on taking back responsibility could be taught and learned in effective ways and would lay the foundation for a Dogrib justice system.

Considerable community education is required to reach agreement on using Dene traditional rules for social control in ways that are enforceable because consensus has not yet been reached. A facilitator could work with DJP Dogrib staff and leadership to build consensus over a period of one year through community workshops and individual contacts.

3. *After consensus is reached, the Lac La Martre people need to form their own Dogrib justice committee and to establish a pilot project to test old and new Dogrib rules in resolving current "crimes" in the community.*

The justice committee should include members representing both young adults and elders and men and women. Its' task would be to determine how to reestablish workable Dogrib ways of dealing with inappropriate behaviour.

At the beginning, the justice committee should seek to have all incidents referred to it prior to any police or court action. The committee also needs to determine what criteria it will use for selecting cases to handle in the beginning. The eventual goal would be to handle all cases. As well, the committee needs to document what cases are taken, how they are dealt with, and what problems arise from dealing with them in that way. Both successful and unsuccessful outcomes should be recorded. This will help other Dogrib communities wanting to set up their own justice committees.

The enforcement of decisions made by the committee will also have to be dealt with. It would be useful to establish a camp on one of the islands, staffed by elders and a younger couple. This camp could receive people who are not behaving appropriately or not following the instructions of the committee. Adults and youth could learn how to behave "properly" and also get back in touch with their Dene roots.[3]

Finally, in order for this to happen, negotiations will need to take place between the community and the NWT Department of Justice and Justice Canada about turning over power and authority for judicial

---

3   Likely two camps, in different places, might be set up so that youths and adults are separated. It may be that the Dogrib people might prefer to keep men and women separated rather than divided by age. The idea of outbound camps was discussed but the details were not.

decision-making, for diversion of cases prior to charges, and for the establishment and funding of the committee and camps. NWT Justice already has many policy initiatives in place to encourage community participation in the non-Dene system, such as the justice of the peace program, youth committees and justice committees.

The NWT Department of Justice also recognizes that its system has not been ideal for NWT citizens and has committed itself to "serve all residents in a manner which recognizes and respects the constitutional and collective rights of aboriginal persons."[4] The same document indicates it can exercise its mandate "by negotiating justice projects at the community level" and suggests ways this can be accomplished. These new initiatives are commendable.

4. *Any pilot project should run at least two years in order to make sure that the Dogrib system can work, has community support, and can create enforceable new rules for current times.*

The community suggested a pilot project be put in place, which would include the healing process, the community education process, the establishment of a Dogrib Justice committee, and the establishment of bush camps.

Such a pilot project will require resources, both human and financial. We suggest the employment of a full-time facilitator to set the community education process in place, to build consensus, and to work with the Dogrib justice committee when it is formed. The DJP Dogrib staff could work with the facilitator on these activities and eventually take them over. They could be responsible for documenting the process and its results.

Funding could come from several sources. Some funds might also be diverted from current non-Dene justice programs because, as the Dogrib system begins to work, it should save the non-Dene system many dollars. It is our belief that deviant behaviour will be significantly reduced in direct relation to the decrease in alcohol abuse. The healing process, which follows the attainment of sobriety, should promote self-confidence and increase personal responsibility, and responsibility for others.

---

4 Cited from a policy statement, "Community Justice Initiatives in the NWT," NWT Department of Justice, 1991.

5. *If the pilot project is successful, funds should be in place for the Dogrib justice committee to continue its work.*

A commitment to start the process through the establishment of a community education program and the formation of a Dogrib justice committee should imply a long-term commitment by the community and non-Dene justice agencies to following through. Unless that commitment is in place, it seems foolish to start.

It may be that some components of the process appeal more to various agencies and funders than others. Care should be taken not to put things in place unless consensus has been reached by those involved. If the whole community is not on board, the project will fail. This is particularly true if leadership is neither strong nor sober. It would be better to wait than to start in the middle.

The project could be a joint venture between the Lac La Martre Band Council, NWT Justice, Aboriginal Justice Directorate, DCI, and maybe AINA.

Since considerable interest was expressed by other Dogrib communities about seeing similar activities started in their communities, it would be worth while to form a regional Dogrib justice council following the establishment of the Lac La Martre justice committee. Such a council could give support to Lac La Martre and might give advice on more complex cases. In any event, members could learn from association with the Lac La Martre people and then establish their own local programs.

What should the Lac La Martre people do to start the process of change?

There has to be some reality about the way things will go, what changes will be possible now and later, and how much negotiation needs to take place before things change.

No one expects any of the people in the non-Dene justice systems to simply withdraw and let the Dogrib people do their own thing. That would be neither wise nor fair. The Dogrib leadership and elders, and their new justice committee, will have to learn how to run their own affairs again and this will take time.

The research team proposed a long-term goal of a Dogrib justice system. It will take many years to evolve, to negotiate, and to fund. There will be opposition and many hurdles to overcome. It will take considerable time for the Dogrib people to think through and reach consensus about what parts of the old ways will still work and what will have to be created anew.

It will also take time for people involved in the non-Dene system to let go, so the Dogrib people can regain control. However, there are many people in the non-Dene system who will encourage and assist the Dogrib people in accomplishing their goals. The NWT Justice policy statement clearly shows that the NWT Department of Justice is supportive of any Dogrib initiatives that will improve the justice system for people in the NWT. The Minister has committed himself to looking at the proposals for change.

The joint partners in the Traditional Dene Justice Project, DCI, AINA, and Lac La Martre Band Council are clearly interested in seeing a pilot project put in place. We will be available for advice and consultation during the transition and planning period. DCI has a mandate to further Dene cultural growth and development. The proposed pilot project and the recommendations contained within this report fit comfortably into the DCI mandate for the next five-year plan approved by the Dene regional board members. We think the process will be exciting and productive.

What do people do until things change?

The eventual formation of a Dogrib justice committee in the community, following the attainment of consensus and sobriety, can serve several purposes. It means most Territorial Court cases could be diverted from the courts to the community to handle as soon as the committee is established.

The establishment of a bush camp for youth could be truly helpful in keeping young people in the community. It could also be used for adult offenders who have not committed serious crimes.

The community has just been allocated a fine-option program (1994) so many of the minor "crimes," especially those relating to non-payment of fines, can now be resolved with community service. Appropriate Dogrib supervision needs to be developed, rather than that by the non-Dene untrained social worker.

If a Dogrib justice committee were in place, it could ask to do the sentencing on cases not turned over to them for decisions. The sentencing could be done the Dogrib way, that is, in the circle. Territorial and federal judges would have to commit themselves to accepting the recommendations of the elders without alteration.

The goal of the transition period is to gain more control over one's own life and to use that power in the interests of the community. It is important that the Lac La Martre Dogrib justice committee members develop strategies for coping with the transition period by helping out the courts on issues that have to be dealt with by the non-Dene system at this time. However, safeguards should be in place to ensure that the Dogrib justice committee is not coopted by the non-Dene system's "adaptations" and that they continue to pursue their own goals of a totally Dogrib system.

The goal is not to take on non-Dene functions in a non-Dene court but to take on more and more responsibility for community social control and well-being. As the community achieves this goal, the non-Dene courts will have less and less to do and, eventually, could turn everything back to the community. Obviously, the non-Dene justice system should not abandon the Dogrib people until their system is in place and has been proven to be adequate to the tasks they have set out in the pilot project.

The transitions from one system to the other will not necessarily be easy or smooth; much negotiation for power and control and funding will have to take place. However, if there is good political will and mutual respect, these consultations will lead to the eventual withdrawal of non-Dene systems and the establishment of Dene ones. It could be a win-win situation for all parties if the consultations are serious and mutually supportive. However, the process and its success are dependent on some of the factors identified in the report, such as sobriety on the Dogribs' part and the willingness to give up power, control, and money on the non-Denes' part.

We think the establishment of a Dogrib justice pilot project would work well in Lac La Martre and would lead eventually to the "taking back" of Dene justice throughout Denendeh. This would be a major accomplishment.

Reflections on Selected Literature

This discussion of some of the literature is based on a selected set of materials written by anthropologists, criminologists, lawyers, and various other scholars who have addressed the issues of aboriginal justice. The bibliography is comprehensive and covers the major areas of concern in aboriginal justice. I have tried to select the most relevant writings, and the most recent.

I have attempted to consolidate the bibliography around major questions that arose during the period of the research or might arise in discussions in the future. I have classified these as: 1) ethnographic issues that relate to the past and the present lives of the Dene; 2) the counterpoint between Dene traditional legal concepts and practices and those of the non-Dene; 3) philosophical, moral, and political contentions that may create conflict between Dene and non-Dene propositions for a justice system. I did not include the multitude of criminological and sociological studies with their abysmal lists of statistics regarding native incarceration and recidivism in Canada but have selected a few key works.

I have tried to keep the focus on what we can learn from Dene traditional knowledge and its application which could inform and underlie future planning for self-determination in all phases of life, including social control.

1. Ethnographic Issues

Many social scientists choose to distinguish between "tradition" and "custom." I prefer to see them as an integrated process that encapsulates the continuity between generations, conceptual continuity, and persistence of cultural practices. If one perceives traditions and customs of a specific cultural group as the bases on which the society operates, we can logically assume that embedded in them are the institutional pragmatics and practices that reflect social organization holistically. This would, of necessity, include the legal concepts and practices that constitute the rules of the group.

Webster (1981) defines "custom" as:

> a form or course of action which is characteristically repeated under like circumstances; a usage or practice common to many; a long-established, continued, peaceable, reasonable, certain, and constant practice considered as unwritten law and resting for authority on long consent; a usage that has by long continuance acquired a legally binding force.

Further, Webster (1981) defines "tradition" as:

> a process of handing down information, opinions, beliefs and customs by word of mouth or by example; transmission of knowledge and institutions through sucsessive generations without written instruction; a cultural continuity embodied in a massive complex of evolving social attitudes, beliefs, conventions, and institutions rooted in the experience of the past and exerting an orienting and normative influence on the present.

Thus, we see that the two definitions reflect social realities in the sense that repetitive actions, based on consensus over time, not only acquire a legal force but also emerge from past experience, passed down orally; this cultural continuity not only evolves but exerts a "normative" influence on the present.

It is has been documented throughout the book that traditional knowledge and behaviour had their roots in a system of beliefs that was holistic, the values of which are equally appropriate today, but the practices of which were forestalled from natural evolution by colonialism and the overlay of beliefs, practices, and institutions of the dominant society. If that overlay were removed, the considerable living memory of traditional ways among the Dene would reassert itself. Therefore, evolution could continue and could likely provide the basis for a contemporary Dene system of social control, i.e., a Dene justice system.

Helm and Gillespie (1981:9) state:

> In terms of cultural idiom and perspectives, only since the 1950s have the Dogrib as a people begun to move beyond oral tradition as the sole vehicle of their own perceived history.

Vansina and Carmack, cited by Helm and Gillespie (1981) indicate:

> The histories of people at this level of sociocultural integration (i.e., band or micro-societies) are generally dismissed as neither having a sense of linear time nor embodying historical realities. Yet as independently verified by the Euroamerican record since about 1770 ... within their oral traditions Dogribs evidence a firm comprehension of both historical realities and their temporal succession.

Not only do the Dene people have traditional knowledge, but they also have a firm sense of the "right ways of doing things." These ways constitute a set of rules that were taught and practised through many generations. They are the body of "laws" for Dene society.

As Rasing (1984:1) notes: "It appears that the use of the law concept is a deep-rooted tradition in legal anthropology, starting with the 19th century evolutionists."

Berket-Smith (1929:260ff.) was the first to coin the phrase "customary law," which, according to him, "contained no explicit legal rules but [did contain] behavioural norms generated through custom, public opinion deciding what is or what is not admissible." Cited in Rasing (1984:5), he claims: "the legal rules do not aim to achieve justice as we know it, but to maintain peace and order."

In contemporary Canadian laws, community standards guide judges in their assessment of breaches of those laws, which are based on norms passed down through generations. The Dene are no different in their judgments of what is right and wrong according to their long-established traditional customs.

However, the explicitness of the Dogrib rules is documented in this book. People defined normative behaviour, decided what actions breached those norms, and could explain why those breaches were harmful to both the individual and the collective. If one accepts these early definitions of what constituted "law," by any standard, it is clear that the ways laws are evolved, defined, and applied are culturally defined.

The function of laws, rather than their forms, needs to be acknowledged and accepted. As we indicated, the balance and reciprocities between human, animal, plant, and spiritual worlds determined the survival of the group. Thus, the socialization of younger generations by elders was based on passing down proper ways of doing things as well as the knowledge about the ramifications of not following the rules.

According to Hoebel (1954:28), two conditions must be met before law can be determined: 1) a legitimate authority, and 2) the fear of (physical) coercion (cited in Rasing, 1984:9). These criteria are met in the case of the Dogrib. Many elders' stories detailed the authority of the *yabahti*, which was softened by consensus. Lac La Martre people indicated that people no longer "feared" the leaders as an explanation for the failure of Dogrib rules to work now.

The separation of the application of "law" from its socio-economic, religious, and cultural components is one characteristic that distinguishes Canadian legal processes from those of the Dogrib and other aboriginal peoples. However, the holistic nature of the Dene worldview is damaged by dealing with things separately. We separated resource rules from family and political ones in order to have an understandable text, but they are all one piece of the fabric of Dogrib reality.

This compartmentalizing dilemma is addressed by an Alaskan Dene, Andrew Chapeskie (1990:189), when he commented on the Alaska Native Claims Settlement Act of 1971. He said:

> In the old days no one would have dreamed of laying claim to the land. It belonged not just to the Dene but to the moose, caribou, bears and birds as well. The river was shared by the fish in it and the people on it.

He goes on to comment on the conflict between the indigenous traditional use of lands and the mega-exploitation of resources by the State and the Canadian government through the regulatory processes, and through resource extraction. He states (1990:193ff.):

> The prejudice has been pervasive enough such that there has been often a tendency even to deny the existence of indigenous resource management regimes and their attendant customary laws.... Tragically, this represents a primitive understanding of indigenous societies by Western societies where many question whether or not indigenous societies can survive ... it remains the tragedy of Euro-Canadian jurisprudence in particular that, generating a recognition of indigenous customary law has been, and remains, an extremely difficult and tortuous process that has only just begun.

There is no doubt that many Canadians deny, or do not believe, that indigenous peoples had laws. Generally, people may not recognize the many traditional rules that are still in use and certainly may not recognize them as "laws." This research has been dedicated to trying to document Dogrib rules and the ways in which they were taught and passed down from generation to generation, the spiritual connections on which they were based, and the reciprocities that existed among all of earth's living things, spirits, and peoples.

It is important, therefore, that we continue the explanation so people can recognize where these rules came from and how they worked.

Social Organization of Hunting and Trapping Subsistence Groups

In order to provide the context for the identification of the rules or laws that maintained the Dogrib society from time of living memory, it might be useful to reflect on the ways in which hunting and trapping societies were organized for subsistence and survival.

Northern existence is difficult, and it is not surprising that there are tales of "pitiful" times when people died of starvation or disease. For those who survived hard times and lived to exist in current times, it would seem that survival was based on firm wisdom and pragmatic approaches to difficulties. Examining how people coped, not only with the environment but with each other, is to learn about strength and endurance, as well as wisdom.

These characteristics of personal and social strength should not be eclipsed by the overwhelming body of literature on social pathology, alcohol abuse, physical abuse, and incarceration. So little has been written about the strength of generations that I hope this document will lead people to think about how and why Dene culture not only continues to survive but actually flourishes in some places. This is not to say that anyone should, or could, return to the past and its hardships, but rather to ask what of the past could strengthen and direct the present and future.

Subsistence was based on a seasonal round of activities, which required considerable mobility in order to obtain food and fish, medicinal plants, and, eventually, furs for trade. Settlement came with the ingress of trading posts, missionaries, schools, health centres, and permanent housing. In spite of these changes, and the relatively rapid acculturation that took place, people continue to be somewhat mobile and often travel by plane, snowmobile, with dogs, and by canoe to obtain food, furs and plants. The linkages to the land remain.

Fundamental changes in subsistence life-styles are noted by Helm and Gillespie (1981) to have begun to change only in the 1950s. My own experiences with the Dogrib people at Lac La Martre in the late 1950s supports Helm's observations. At that time, people gathered in summer at the present community but still spent most of the winter out on the land. People lived in tents, although a few families had log cabins out on the land and in the present town-site.

Trapping fur-bearers for cash and trade was the primary economic activity while hunting, fishing, and gathering provided food and hides for jackets, footwear, and mitts. People were poor in an economic sense but rich in spiritual ways and connected to each other through kinship alliances and partnerships.

The environment in which the Dogribs lived traditionally, and continue to inhabit today, is primarily boreal forest of spruce, tamarack, and willow, punctuated by many lakes and rivers. There is intermittent permafrost. In the past, this land provided wood, medicine, logs for houses and caches, and large game, small game, and fur bearers. There are several species of migratory birds that are taken in spring and fall. As well, people hunted caribou in the barren lands.

The major gathering place was old Ft. Rae, and contemporary Rae-Edzo continues to be a major meeting place. Territorial boundaries were flexible and hunters and trappers often met other Dene people on the trail. Vanstone (1974:47) notes that 1,200 Dogrib gathered at Ft. Rae, once the trading post was established at the turn of the century.

The climatic conditions under which people lived varied from highs of ninety degrees Fahrenheit in summer to minus fifty Fahrenheit in winter. Fall and spring climates were moderate. Wind affected people as well, adding major wind-chill factors in winter but bringing welcome relief from mosquitoes and black flies in summer. Reports of people freezing to death in winter are noted, as are some drownings in fall and spring storms. The long twenty-four-hour light made June and July comfortable and pleasant times for fishing, gathering, and visiting.

As Savishinsky (1974:37) notes for the Ft. Good Hope people:

> The fact that people's calendar is a description rather than a demarcation of time reflects their concern with the natural world, and serves as a mirror of their own participation in it ... survival is a challenge rather than an assumption.

He notes, as we do for the Dogrib, that the traditional reliance on game and migratory fowl was counterbalanced by the scarcity of edible roots, plants and berries. This ecological fact meant that people had to work very hard for their subsistence and that the unpredictability of caribou migrations added to the anxiety of hunters and trappers. In the past, it also added to greater mobility.

Mobility, the need for food, and, eventually, the desire for fur bearers to trade meant that people were separated from each other for long periods of time. Kinship alliances were bilateral; that is, people chose their partners and camp co-residents from either their mother's or their father's side. This pattern is common to most hunting and trapping groups. It would seem from information obtained and from observation that the kinship preference is patrilineal; that is, men determine political relationships and structure camps and activities with male kin.

However, the residence pattern is matrilocal since men live in the communities, and sometimes the parental households, of the women they marry. The importance of kinship in structuring social relationships rested in the need for hunting and trapping partners and for marriages that would provide greater access to hunting and trapping territories and increased political alliances in the event of wars between neighbouring tribal groups. A bilateral system provides this greater range of choice.

"Family" was, and remains, the basic unit of social interaction. While most people now live in nuclear family units, most households accommodate two to three generations of kin. This residential pattern is reflective of the traditional camps where a senior male family head was the *k'àowo* and the camp consisted mainly of his adult sons and daughters and their spouses and children.

As Savishinsky (1974:68) notes:

> It [the camp] contains each person's closest kinsmen, and so it is also the locus of the strongest affective ties in each individual's social spheres. It involves the people among whom bonds of generosity, interdependence, and mutual aid are the strongest, and social relations exhibit a combination of warmth, respect and restraint. The respect that children show for their parents, and the bonds that siblings establish with one another, ideally continue into the children's adulthood, thus perpetuating the family's cohesiveness over time.

Traditionally, these social arrangements were effective in protecting the group from hunger or abandonment. The distribution of food ensured everyone was fed, and the shift of children from nuclear families to extended ones through adoption ensured that both children and elders had companions, respect, and someone to care for them over many years. These patterns of behaviour are observable today but are not always consistent. The important point is that the values on which the behaviour was based still could be used to revitalize relationships and responsibility one for the other.

As McDonnell (1992a:v) notes for the James Bay Cree hunter and trappers:

> ... people are culturally defined as interdependent. The effect is to integrate members of the group by insisting that every contribution is partial; it requires others for its completion.... Social order in a hunting setting, therefore, may be usefully thought of as integrating differences.... Being a member of a hunting group was, in this sense, being a participant in a moral order that viewed the person not as equivalent to the group, but as a contributor to the collective well-being of the group as a whole.

Asch (1982:359) writing about the Slavey, but generalizing to all Dene, contends:

> the traditional institutional and value framework of Dene hunting-gathering remained little changed well into the 1970s. For example, within the primary unit of production and consumption, labour was still organized solely on the basis of age and sex. As well, hunting-gathering still relied on methods of game capture that are labour-intensive and required collective action. Further, reciprocity still obtained within the household and, indeed, where surpluses existed this practice was routinely extended to other households in the community.

This documentation is important because there is a tendency among members of Canadian society to view hunting and trapping activities, perceptions, and values as residual ones left over from traditional times, as recreation and irrelevant to modern ones. However, hunting and trapping are viable economic and subsistence activities that still provide substantial amounts of food, jackets, footwear, and mitts, still allow for reciprocity, and still link generations of kin to the land and to each other. As well, they maintain the spiritual connection to the land.

Animal power was one of the most important connections to the spirit world because it gave one access to animals. Vanstone (1974:65) notes that:

> the Dogrib believed that since men and women could be reincarnated in animal form, animals could understand what humans said.... All Athapaskans had numerous taboos ... that applied to food and hunting. Nearly all of these were designed to prevent the animals' spirits from being offended and to make sure that important game remained plentiful.

The many accounts we collected during interviews on the rules for hunting, trapping, fishing, and gathering confirm various accounts in the literature for Athapaskan hunting and trapping societies. As well, the accounts underline the fact that these beliefs, practices, and rules still exist.

Transitions and Change

As noted above, Ft. Rae was the traditional gathering place for the Dogrib people. Until settlement took place from the 1950s on, people from Rae Lakes, Snare Lakes, and other hunting and trapping camps within the Dogrib territories tended to gather once or twice a year. The trading post was established about 1790 and marshalled in the fur trade, consumer goods, guns, traps, and other material goods.

The first major impact was the exchange of furs for goods and cash. In 1852, a Hudson's Bay Company post opened at the old Ft. Rae and then moved to the present Rae-Edzo site about 1921 when Monfwi signed

Treaty 11. This allowed the HBC fur trade to flourish without the competition of the Northern Trading Company, which had also settled at Ft. Rae in 1890. It is reported that close to 600 Dogrib trappers traded at the HBC post at that time.

The first doctor came into the area in 1900 and visited annually after that, but measles, tuberculosis, and influenza took their toll in the 1920s and 1930s. One report indicates that by 1940 it was felt that the Dogrib people were on their way to extinction (Dene Nation Crime Prevention Project 1989:24). A hospital was established by the Roman Catholic missionaries in 1940, electricity arrived in the 1950s, and the connector road to the Mackenzie Highway opened in 1960.

The Dogrib people began to settle in their fishing or hunting sites, preparing the way for sedentary communities and more material amenities such as permanent housing, electricity, water service, health centres, schools, churches, police, courts, and local formal governments. These changes had major ramifications for the quality of life, the relationships between Dene and non-Dene, and the change of life styles. We will focus here primarily on the shift from Dogrib forms of social control to non-Dene ones, that is, the overlay of Western legal concepts and practices, the evolution of the NWT court system, and the shifting of responsibilities for social control from Dogrib leaders to the RCMP.

2. Counterpoint: Dene justice system and non-Dene ones

Earlier chapters of the book provide sufficient details about the nature of Dene systems of social control. Here, the focus is on the problems associated with the overlay of non-Dene systems on Dene ones. This overlay seemingly has been put in place without much understanding on the part of the non-Dene about the ramifications of changing the contexts of social control. As Patenaude (1989:1) notes:

> The imposition of incursive law and legal systems has often been accomplished with neither recognition of existing indigenous systems nor concern for the results of that imposition.... Recently, our work has noted increased concern about the effectiveness of adversarial systems of criminal justice, particularly where these systems have been imposed on cultures which have traditionally utilized mediation, negotiation and other forms of dispute resolution.

After the period of contact, social control was removed from the Dogrib leaders and assumed by the RCMP and missionaries. The reasons why this was accomplished so easily have been stated earlier (p. 58ff.).

Initially, misdemeanors were dealt with by the RCMP, who charged the individual, judged and sentenced him or her, and, if convicted, incarcerated the person in RCMP cells in the regional centre, i.e., Ft. Rae. More serious crimes resulted in arrests, detention, and arraignment locally, transportation to Alberta for trial, sentencing, and imprisonment.

In 1955, John Sissons became the first judge of the Territorial Court of the Northwest Territories (Bucknell 1967:159). Sissons felt that:

> The proper place for a trial is the place where the offence was committed or the cause of the action arose; every person accused of a serious offence is entitled to be tried by a jury drawn from the area in which the offence was committed, and no man shall be condemned except by the judgment of his peers and the law of the land.

Sissons' belief in these rules of law led to the formation of the Circuit Courts and to the adaptation of some local customary law into the non-Dene system, most notably marriage (Noah: 1962, 36 W.W.R. 577) and adoption (Katie: 1962, 38 W.W.R. 100). It is also noteworthy that not many of Sissons' southern colleagues agreed with his judicial interpretations of local issues, nor with his judgments, especially those involving game laws. Many were overturned in the Appeal Courts and in the Supreme Court.

Sissons' contributions were emulated by W.C. Morrow, who became the next judge of the Territorial Court. Bucknell points out Sissions made his mark not by what he did but by how he did it. He notes (1967:160):

> In his judicial role, Sissons merged a profound reverence for ancient legal tradition with an unique ability to adapt those traditions to the challenges of new situations. In his eyes, the law did not exist above society, but within society; it must be tested and retested against the demands society made upon it.

There is no doubt that Sissons and Morrow were sensitive to the differences of cultures. There is also no doubt that they believed that the non-Dene system was superior to that of the Inuit and Dene, and they worked hard to educate people in the communities about the benefits of the new legal system.

Morrow notes that the name change from "Territorial Court" to "Supreme Court" was made in 1978 and that the three magistrates became territorial "judges," thus bringing the northern court system into the two-level system reflective of the south (Morrow 1981:381). By 1960, an Appeal Court had been established in the NWT, and, in 1971, the GNWT took over responsibility for the court system, but the Crown's office remains under the federal Department of Justice.

Morrow discusses the difficulties of acculturation proceeding at an uneven pace, resulting in the fact that some communities were familiar with the court process and others were not. He states (1981:384):

If the court party finds it is about to commence a hearing in a settlement where there has been little recent exposure to legal process, the judge will take considerable care to explain in his opening remarks what the court system is all about, how each participant is expected to do his part, and so on. It is a standing rule of the Supreme Court to make provision for two court interpreters – one for the court and one for the accused. The defence interpreter is instructed to monitor the court's interpreter to see that the story is properly brought out. He or she is instructed to speak out if there is any difficulty, and it has happened.

It is interesting to note that the court recognized that people did not understand the court process nor the role of court officers and that interpreters were essential to the process of both educating the community and running a fair trial.

Current complaints documented throughout the project about the non-Dene system in communities now presumed to be familiar with the courts and their legal processes continue to reflect major problems in understanding those very things. Judges seldom explain much and trained interpreters are seldom on hand. As well, the courts are still seen as an imposition on Dene life, especially in the precise area which Sissons tried hardest to adapt: family law.

Morrow raises an interesting point (1981:384) when he states: "I am not convinced that the average native does not still feel he should confide in the local investigating officer."

While Morrow sees this tendency in the context of alcohol charges where the person in a drunken state may say anything or may not remember what he did or said, I am more inclined to interpret such behaviour as an adhesion to traditional values. That is, the person knows what he has done, knows that the community members know, and acknowledges his wrong-doing in order to begin to restore harmony, etc. The intervention of defence counsel at that point, or the judge's refusal to accept a guilty plea, is seen by community people as a denial of their ways of doing things, and it removes any community responsibility to the accused for the healing process.

Morrow takes credit for himself and Sissons "in preserving the culture" (1981:387) with reference to custom marriage and custom adoption. This is not the perception of the Supreme Court held by the Lac La Martre people who were angry at its intrusion into the Apple-Bishop custody case, which they considered was a family matter to be resolved by the families.

It seems it is difficult for the judiciary and lawyers to understand that making a ruling that is consonant with existing local custom is not necessarily preserving, nor understanding, the cultural issues. The judgment in itself is an intrusion into the culture that is not appreciated. Because the overlaid system arrives at some decisions that are the same as those of the community does not affirm the latter. Nor is legal affirmation of their decisions necessarily wanted by the community.

Finally, Morrow places great pride in having selected local juries for four rape cases, one of which, historically, was composed of only women, and none of which convicted the men. Current juries don't seem much inclined to convict in rape cases either. He reports the use of a jury as a great success in contributing to a major murder trial at Spence Bay where two individuals took part in a medicine fight (R. v. Shooyuk; unreported 1966; jury verdicts in NWT, Alberta Law Review, 1970).

The case is a nice example of the questionable overlay of the non-Inuit legal system since the community anguished over what to do with a woman who was destroying their hunting camp. The Inuit interpretation of her state was that she was possessed by bad spirits; Morrow says she was mentally ill. Since no one could control her, and all the members of the hunting party might perish if she totally destroyed the camp, a decision was made by the elders that the senior hunter would kill her. In order to avoid a feud, the woman's son accompanied him to ensure that there were no other alternatives and that she had to be killed. She was shot; it was 1961. People then retrieved what they could and moved camp.

Two years later, a RCMP patrol came through and the senior hunter handed him a full description of the matter, written in syllabics. The officer eventually passed it on and a charge of murder was laid against the hunter, Shooyuk, and the younger man (the son), Ayaak. Both agreed they had done it and a plea of "guilty" was entered. The jury – all Inuit – found Shooyuk "guilty" of manslaughter and found Ayaak "not guilty." Because of the evidence, Morrow gave Shooyuk a suspended sentence, and he was allowed to return to his hunting camp.

Morrow remarks that without a jury, the judge would have had to find both men guilty of murder. One has to wonder why the non-Inuit court had to intervene in a situation that was already settled in the Inuit way, especially when it resulted in the same ending: Shooyuk and Ayaak returned to their camps to continue their lives. One also has to wonder what the Inuit felt and thought at being called for jury duty five years after the fact when they had kin who had already participated in a collective and difficult decision to end the woman's life.

Lac La Martre had its first jury trial in 1993 for the Simpson-Zoe sexual abuse case. Selection of the jury created great anguish in the community and some people expressed considerable anxiety about assuming that role because they felt it was not their way of doing things. That is, some felt there was insufficient time to discuss the issue, the rules for procedure were non-Dene, no opportunity was given the victim to sit in the circle, no opportunity was given the accused to sit in the circle, male-female issues were compressed into curious molds, and interpretation was dubious. The old rule of law of judgment by peers might more usefully be exercised in the circle and in the language of the group.

Lillies (1989:3) indicates that the criminal justice system has a disproportionate impact on natives compared to non-natives, in Canada generally, as well as in the many small isolated communities in the north where Indian and Inuit populations are significant.

He notes (Lillies 1989:6) that: "Residents of northern communities, and in particular the native population, are particularly susceptible to being "improperly" incarcerated for fine default." We have noted the shared concerns of the Lac La Martre people about the same issue. The establishment of a fine-option program began in July 1994 in Lac La Martre, and it is hoped that it will resolve this conflict between the two ways of doing things in the future.

Lillies (1989:9) also notes that the matter of equality before the law presumes that there is cultural homogeneity that operates to maintain the existing sociocultural order. He asserts that this assumption is patently false and says:

> The equal treatment by the justice system of those native people who are culturally and otherwise distinctive is, at best, problematic and, at worst, discriminatory.... In these communities, the probability of systematic cultural bias impacting on decision-making at all stages of the criminal justice system is significantly greater than in larger populations.

Lillies then proceeds to compare value systems of natives and non-natives with the aim of showing that misinterpretation of behaviour and characteristics can lead to inappropriate assessments and decisions. Rupert Ross (1992:6–10) emphasizes similar points in his section on "signals of difference." Lowe (1985:6) calls circuit courts "wrist-watch justice" and elaborates points made earlier about the dearth of time the court party, and defence counsel especially, spend in the community and the little understanding and knowledge people have even after many years of court parties going to the same communities.[1]

---

1 I recall observing the first court party to come in after my arrival in Lac La Martre in 1991. Court was held in Hamlet Council Chambers. The Court party walked through the crowd of Dogrib people waiting for their mail; no one stopped, looked at, or greeted any of the Dogribs. At lunch time, the Court party ate their lunch in Chambers and no one went outside. Court proceeded without an interpreter; the

The Lac La Martre experience shows that many lawyers and some judges still do not understand, or at least fail to acknowledge, that lack of eye contact, lack of emotion, and failure to appear, do not mean a lack of respect for the court or lack of remorse. On the contrary, it is still unacceptable for most Dogrib people to look strangers in the eye, to talk loudly to them, or to show emotion in front of them. And the court party is always composed of "strangers."

Behaviour changes when people become less strange; that is, when Lac La Martre people begin to get to know "strangers," they can be very expressive. This was confirmed when the Crown prosecutor began coming in a day before the court party when he could. He was able to get to know some of the people informally, and they responded by both talking to him and seeking advice from him.

A final counterpoint that seems useful to comment on, and which is raised by Ross (1992:6-10) for the Ojibwa, is the way the courts proceed with their adversarial system, which is in opposition to the Dene ways of thinking about and doing things. In the non-Dene courts, there are accused and witnesses; lawyers represent defence and prosecution; that is, they are on opposing sides. Evidence is given about the accused in his or her presence. The language used is English, and sometimes interpretation is available. Minor cases take a few minutes; others take longer. The accused is asked to plead guilty or not guilty. If found guilty, the accused is sentenced, which means she or he is punished. That ends it. It is all done by strangers.

All of this is culturally offensive. As noted previously, witnesses cringe at testifying against a person. The circle where "harsh words" are said are aimed at teaching the person what he or she did wrong and how to correct it – after the miscreant has acknowledged responsibility for the offensive behaviour. No one talks about the character of the person, only about the behaviour; motives are not imputed. It may take days or weeks to resolve the matter. The important thing is that time is taken to come to a full

---

physical arrangements allowed the court party to talk to each other, but made it difficult for community people to hear. Defence counsel spent about three to five minutes with each client and one sensed she was under tremendous pressure from the rest of the court party to get through her interviews so court could proceed. Court lasted two and a half hours and the court party left without ever having "connected" with any Dogrib people, or having seen the community or patronized the local cafe. It seemed an amazing feat of encapsulation! Later, things changed; the court moved to the community hall or the school; some judges rearranged the physical setting so community members could hear and see; the court party began to arrange for lunch at the cafe and some began to walk around and talk to people informally.

understanding of why (not how) the person did the misdeed. People are not on any side, they surround the person, and the victim is part of the circle. The discussions are in the local language, and no one defends the victim or the accused. Everyone is there to discuss, to find out what has happened, to start the healing process. There are ramifications, depending on what the person has done, but more emphasis is placed on what he or she is prepared to do to remedy the situation. The person is not punished; he or she is helped. Stories are told to give the person guidance. The people in the circle are friends and relatives; they have to live together. Every person's wisdom counts.

Ross (1992:58-9) illustrates the contradictions that arise between the two cultural systems. He describes the case of a drunken man who viciously assaulted his wife. In court, the male leadership spoke of him positively and said he had helped his family, had not been drinking, and was ashamed of his behaviour. They asked that he not be sent to jail so he could remain in the community where they would continue to help him heal. Ross, as Crown counsel, urged the judge to sentence the man to jail so that a message would be sent to other men that they should not act violently. The judge concurred and, as the accused waited by the plane, fifteen women came to wish him well, to hug him, and to talk to him. Ross suggests that such behaviour by the women recognized the fact that they knew he would return to the community when his jail term was finished and that he should not feel reviled by the women. If he did, he might become violent again. If they demonstrated their for-giveness and the promise of a welcome home, he might heal sufficiently so as not to become violent again. The community response implied no judgment of the accused, the judge, or the lawyer.

Ross concludes (1992:98) that the majority society should adopt some of the views of the aboriginal society. He notes: "These include respect for the natural sphere, an emphasis upon careful and sensitive consensus-build-ing, a focus upon rehabilitative and preventive response to social turmoil."

3. Philosophical, moral, and political issues in contemporary Dene and non-Dene worlds. Is there a meeting point now or in the future?

Reference has been made to the process of acculturation that began with the contact period and the arrival of non-Dene in Denendeh. Initially, the impact was not great, but eventually the loss of bush skills, inter-dependence, and reciprocity in Dene relationships resulted in an increas-ing dependence on non-Dene institutions and people. The availability of alcohol, and its abuse, led to further losses within Dene communities themselves. Children lost their ties with grandparents; grandparents failed to socialize the generation that had been removed and raised in residential schools. Parents didn't know how to parent for a future that was uncertain at best. These changes came very rapidly and not long ago; the 1950s saw the beginning of Dogrib settlement. We noted that many Dogrib people were still in control of their own lives as late as the 1970s. Now the Dogrib people want to reverse the direction of change and resume control of their lives and the functions of the non-Dene institutions and programs that affect them so vitally. Justice is but one of these.

As Ross notes (1992:112):

> There appears to be, in many Native communities today, a concerted ef-
> fort to restore Elders to the elevated position they formerly held within
> each community, to recover both for them and for the community itself
> some of their traditional teachings and practices.

As previously noted, and as Ross comments for the Ojibwa (1992:126ff.):

> It is my guess that the remote northern communities sense that this vision
> [of providing continuity of socialization for the survival of the collective],
> this conviction, is slipping away and that in this critical respect the *order-
> ing of life* is slipping away with it. I sense a fear that life itself, Indian life, is
> seen as threatened by an escalating process of disintegration....
>
> Personal worth was evaluated in terms of the roles one played within
> the continuing family, not in terms of an individual's operating autono-
> mously, selfishly, within a larger society....
>
> By going to our schools children ... may unlearn the morality that tra-
> ditionally forbade cultivating individual egos through competition, praise,
> comparison, censure, reward and punishment.

The recognition that contact and colonialism not only overlaid but also denigrated local cultures raises two points: what do we do to re-store the damage and what do the Dene do to reclaim their lives? Our society has taught children and young adults to be competitive. We have already noted that the qualities of self-reliance and generosity evidenced by respect and sharing among extended family members has been di-minished if not totally obscured by non-Dene institutions such as the school, the mission, the health centre, the courts, and administration. Yet, there remains the traditional knowledge and the desire to retrieve those practices; the Lac La Martre people decided to start with justice and medicine and now are looking at education.

Ross (1992:166ff.) offers a few insights that highlight recommendations made here with regard to transitional measures that might work as people move to take back responsibility for their own ways. He reports a definition of native law given by Ojibwa justice of the peace Charlie Fisher:

> [T]raditional Native common law was comprised of only five words. The first was "Respect" which meant respect for all things, for all people, for the Creator, and for yourself. The next two were "Good" and "Bad." If you learned respect, you would then know what was bad and what was good. The last two words were "Good Life," for if you understood the law and followed it, a good life would be the result.
>
> [Elders] remind [the accused] of how important they are to their family and the community, and about the contributions they can make in the future. They also talk about the help that they and others stand ready to provide to assist each person to realize his or her potential.
>
> The Elders seem to think it is counter-productive to tell an offender constantly how much damage he has done, how he has hurt others, how it is his failure to control his harmful impulses that is to blame. They seem to make a deliberate attempt to improve each offender's self-esteem by reminding him of his potential for goodness, of his capacity to move forward, with help, for self-fulfillment. Their constant emphasis is on respect, *including respect for one's self.*
>
> The quicker a particular mistake is compensated for and forgiven, and the balance thus restored, the quicker each offender can resume his natural progress. From the Native perspective, even the notion of a criminal record is seen as counter-productive, for it serves only to remind of failure.

We see, then, that the Sandy Lake Ojibwa have arrived at conclusions very similar to those of the Lac La Martre Dogrib people. We have documented the same perceptions and traditions here. What is useful to note is the uniformity of perception that the way the courts proceed is not only culturaly offensive but, in fact, is in opposition to the very fundamental values of the "right ways of doing things" among the Dene. Similar conclusions can be drawn from other areas such as the Northwest Coast, where the South Island Tribal Council attempted to reclaim their process by taking it back to the traditionalists in the Salish big houses. They too chose to use spiritual methods to restore harmony within the person and to achieve restitution and closure.[2] Other indigenous groups seem also to be moving in similar directions in Ontario, Manitoba, Saskatchewan, Alberta, and British Columbia.

Other problems with the interface between non-Dene and Dene systems is characterized by Havermann's (1989:61) commentary on the

---

2 Island Justice; personal communication with Tom Samson, Director and Judge Doug Campbell, 1991-93.

linkages within the non-Dene system between the court, the police, and social services. Our observations are similar. He notes:

> The policing of indigenous communities appears to fulfill a hybrid function of order maintenance and social service to a much greater degree than it does in other communities.... Social indicators of immiseration [sic] coupled with indigenized, social-service-oriented policing of indigenous people highlight the territorial injustice of their treatment by both the waxing exceptional state and the waning welfare state as the fiscal crisis deepens....
>
> The hybridization of social service with crime control has a "net-widening" effect which leads to the extensive incarceration of indigenous people: since police define the problems, police solutions are found. Police are the gatekeepers of the criminal justice system; it is largely their activities which dictate the size of the prison population.

Cloke, cited in Havermann (1989:62) states:

> The mere existence of a unified system of law for two social classes which are ... in opposition ... is itself oppressive. The purpose of such a system of law can only be the regularization of conflict between the two to ensure that differences are always resolved in the interests of the dominant party.

As we noted earlier, the discretionary power of the RCMP was used very differently by Constable Les Dell and Constable Tom Roy, the former preferring to intervene and not charge, the latter choosing to lay charges. The involvement of social services in a variety of cases usually resulted in decisions being made by non-Dene rather than Dene. For example, it was the untrained non-Dene social worker who suggested to Dolphus Apple that he obtain a lawyer and file a custody suit for Sharlene after his parents asked for custom adoption forms. This was done without consultation with senior members of either family or their elders. The custody issue likely could have been resolved in the community before the legalities escalated it into the courts.

Griffiths and Patenaude (1988:5) note:

> in developing policy and programs, the federal, provincial and territorial governments have generally failed to consider the diversity among Native Indian and Inuit communities, to address the causal factors associated with Native conflict with the law, and have retained control over the structure and content of the programs.

Part of the problem involved in such matters is that there is no enabling legislation in Canada that would allow indigenous people to develop and administer their own criminal justice programs. Until recently, any such attempts were resisted, and, in 1992, then-minister of justice Kim Campbell vowed in Whitehorse (and elsewhere) that no separate systems would be allowed to develop. Notwithstanding that pronouncement, the GNWT Department of Justice and the Federal Aboriginal Justice Directorate have both been working quietly toward more sensitive and informed directions of determining what aboriginal peoples might like to do and how their ideas might be implemented within existing policies and through new initiatives.[3]

Changes have been in progress in an attempt to make community-based justice more participatory through the use of elders, establishment of advisory justice committees, community supervised service in lieu of detention, fine-option programs, and the justice of the peace programs. Social services is often the vehicle through which fine-option and community service options are supervised. While these initiatives are laudatory from the point of view of the overlaid criminal justice system, their implementation does not allow the community to resume its responsibility and its own ways of dealing with such issues because the decisions and supervision are in the hands of the non-Dene officials.

Griffiths and Patenaude (1988:15ff.) note the difficulties associated with the community-based programs. They identify the following problems:

1. The dependence of Dene Indian and Inuit communities on "outside" government to initiate, fund, and support community corrections programs.

2. The conflict between traditional Dene Indian and Inuit notions of conflict resolution and those represented by community service order and restitution programs.

3. The operational difficulties of developing and maintaining community service orders and restitution programs in NWT communities.

These views are consonant with those expressed by the Lac La Martre people in the course of the research. One must conclude that "community-based" must be defined as Dene-controlled.

We have noted in several places that non-Dene have difficulty with conceptualizing and accepting the existence of Dene law. Quite apart from individual bias and the majority belief that "our" way is the only "right" way, there are difficulties in contemplating legal pluralism. As Kane (1984:9) notes for Australian aborigines, opposition to the recognition of aboriginal customary law

---

3 See the GNWT policy paper on Aboriginal Justice, 1991.

is sometimes expressed on the grounds that some of its rules are considered repugnant ... and it is desirable to change what seems to be unnecessarily harsh. Another view is that it would be divisive to recognize more than one legal system.... While a pluralist society might be permitted, or even welcome for the purpose of recognizing social and cultural differences, legal pluralism is said to have a potential to create a dual society, even a separate political entity.

Some contend that any attempt to recognize customary law would be to attempt to restore something which has been lost.... We must take care not to create a synthetic law which is neither aboriginal nor Australian.

The same remarks have been heard with reference to the Canadian situation. Additionally, some have commented that a separate system would not protect the principle of "equality" in law and in the criminal justice system. However, we know there is little equality before the law for poor people, people of colour, nor often for women. We also know that in the search for restoration of self-determination that the Constitution has not entrenched that right in real terms of implementation.

The argument here is that the Canadian system of criminal justice generally works for the society that created it – mainly middle- and upper-class whites. It does not work for those whose culture is so different that little common social, political, or economic grounds can be found on which to meet. This is reflected in the dismal statistics of offences and incarceration of aboriginal people. According to Griffiths and Patenaude (1988:22):

in 1985 the NWT had the highest rate of Criminal Code violations [21,345/100,000], the highest rate of violent crime offences [4,288/100,000] and the highest rate of property offences [9,686/100,000] in Canada.

These ratios remain essentially the same today, and the suicide rate is reported to be the highest in Canada.[4]

The judiciary in the Northwest Territories, while expressing some interest in traditional laws of the Dene, seldom credit them with any realistic weight and seem firmly committed to the concept of the same laws applying to all, that is, non-Dene laws. At the Western Judicial Education Workshop held in Yellowknife in 1991, elders and Dogrib researchers met in small groups with the judges. Judges indicated a variety of reactions among which were: "interesting but irrelevant," "archaic," "nonsense," and "there's no going back." A few said it might be interesting to pursue.

---

4 Personal communication, GNWT Department of Justice.

As Kane (1984:14) comments, it might be more useful to consider the issue of indigenous systems, not so much as a question of customary laws, but as a desire to develop more pragmatic means by which Indians themselves might better maintain order in their communities. He concludes with some suggestions that I think might also work in the Northwest Territories (1984:29):

1. Social adherence to the law is greatly enhanced if it is premised upon the local customs of that society; ...

2. Indian people and their representatives should play a central role in identifying and determining the character of the customs and their applicability in the modern context.

3. The notion of a distinctive yet integrated legal process for Indians is consistent with the opportunities offered by Section 107 of the Indian Act and the general approach taken to accommodate the French tradition in Canada.

As Richstone (1983:581) notes:

Cultural diversity and legal pluralism are, moreover, recognized tenets of international law and Canadian constitutional law. Article 27 of the International Covenant of Civil and Political Rights enshrines the "group rights" of ethnic, religious and linguistic minorities and squarely applies to Canada's aboriginal peoples. Section 27 of the Canadian Charter of Rights and Freedoms declares:

This Charter shall be interpreted in a manner consistent with the preservation and enhancement of the multicultural heritage of Canadians.

He concludes (1983:590ff.):

Entrenchment of aboriginal customs and traditions, of its customary law, is not a discrete demand somehow severable from the larger goal of self-development....

In a pluralistic society such as ours, it is not unthinkable to consider that aboriginal peoples, with their manifestly different cultures, have a right to determine their own pace and set their own terms of development. Once this assumption is made, a great deal will follow.

As McDonnell notes for the James Bay Cree (1992b:xiii):

The basis for dealing with social problems ... must be rooted in a moral attitude which might tentatively be characterized as a desire both to give and to receive ... respect. If this is correct then certainly Cree today have an opportunity to reclaim a concept from their own culture that, in its own way, is no less charged with meaning and positive value than "justice" is in the broader Canadian society, and employ this as their guide from the past for the selection and creation of institutions that could better serve them in the present and in the future.

Conclusion

By way of conclusion, let us return to the notion of "justice," which is far more encompassing than that of "criminal justice," or the "legal system," or a "system of rules." Justice implies diversity; it implies that truly just actions arise in the context of culture, language, and community.

The theorists cited above, and many others not cited but included in the bibliography, support the Dogrib view that legal pluralism is not to be avoided if indigenous people are to regain control of the their own communities and lives. People cannot justly be homogenized; competing systems for maintaining social order cannot be rank ordered, if they are to be justly administered. Community standards cannot be developed and enforced if one community dominates another's perception of the "right way of doing things."

The major justice enquiries (Marshall, Manitoba, Alberta) have fully established that the dominant system of criminal justice does not serve indigenous people justly or equally. The challenge now in the Northwest Territories is to be on the cutting edge of exciting new developments, to use traditional values and perspectives of the Dene to face the future, and to work as partners in supporting their ways of doing things for themselves. The joint partners in this project have started on that long trail in very positive ways.[5]

---

5   For those wishing to explore justice initiatives of other First Nations, please see the list and descriptions in Mandamin (1992, v. 2, tabs. 5-8).

Bibliography

Ackman, D. 1985. *Canada-Saskatchewan/FSIN Studies: Justices of the Peace under Section 107 of the Indian Act*. Ottawa: Department of Justice.

Adams, K. Bliss.1988. Order in the courts: Resolution of tribal/state criminal jurisdictional disputes. *Tulsa Law Journal* 24(63).

Adamson, Rebecca. 1992. Investing in indigenous knowledge. *Akwe:kon Journal*.

Alaska Federation of Natives. 1985. *Bush Justice: Policing, Courts, Corrections*. Report on the Fourth Bush Justice Conference, Bethel, Alaska.

Angell, John. 1979. *Alaskan Village Justice: An Exploratory Study*. Anchorage: Criminal Justice Center.

Asch, Michael. 1982. Dene self-determination and the study of hunter-gatherers in the modern world. In: *Politics and History in Band Societies*, ed. Eleanor Leacock and Richard Lee. Cambridge: Cambridge University Press.

Atcheson, Donald. 1978. Canadian native peoples and psychiatric justice. *International Journal of Law and Psychiatry* 1.

Auger, Donald, Anthony Doob, and Raymond Auger. 1992. Crime and justice in three Nishnawbe-Aski Nation communities: An exploratory investigation. *Canadian Journal of Criminology* 34(3/4).

Barsh, Russel Lawrence, and James Youngblood Henderson. 1979. The betrayal: Oliphant *v*. Suquamish Indian Tribe and the hunting of the snark. *Minnesota Law Review* 63.

Bayley, D.H. 1985. *Social control and Political Change*. Research Monograph No. 39, Princeton University thesis, Princeton, New Jersey.

Bayley, John. 1980. Toward the development of a Northwest Territories law reform capability. Unpublished paper. Available from the Northern Justice Centre, Simon Fraser University, Burnaby, B.C.

Bayley, John. 1990. Unilingual aboriginal jurors in a Euro-Canadian criminal system: Some preliminary views of the Northwest Territories experience. Commission on Folk Law and Legal Pluralism, Theme 1. Ottawa: Proceedings of the VI International Symposium.

Bayne, Peter. n.d. Village courts in Papua, New Guinea. Paper presented to the Faculty of Law, Australian National University, Sydney, Australia.

Bell, Diane. 1983. Aboriginal women and the recognition of customary law in Australia. Paper presented to the Department of Anthropology, Australian National University, Sydney, Australia.

Benson, Garry. 1991. Developing crime prevention strategies in aboriginal communities. Paper No. 12. Ottawa: Ministry of the Solicitor General.

Bentzon, Agnete, and Henning Brondstad. 1983. Recognition, repression and transformation of customary law in Greenland during the last 40 years of transition to capitalism. Paper presented to the Commission on Folk Law and Legal Pluralism, Vancouver, B.C.

Berger, Thomas. *A Long and Terrible Shadow: White Values, Native Rights in the Americas, 1492-1992*. Toronto: Douglas & McIntyre, 1991.

Boldt, Menno. 1983. Pre-sentence reports and the incarceration of natives. *Canadian Journal of Criminology* 25.

Boldt, Menno, and Anthony Long. 1984. Tribal philosophies and the Canadian Charter of Rights and Freedoms. *Ethnic and Racial Studies* 7.

Boldt, Menno, J. Long, and Leroy Little Bear, eds. 1986. *The Quest for Justice: Aboriginal Peoples and Aboriginal Rights*. Toronto: University of Toronto Press.

Bonta, James, Jane Boyle, Lawrence Motiuk, and Paul Sonnichsen. 1983. Restitution in correctional half-way houses: Victim satisfaction, attitudes and recidivism. *Canadian Journal of Criminology* 25.

Bouchard, S., and C. Pelletier. 1986. *Justice in Question: An Evaluation of Projects to Create a Local Judiciary in Povungnituk, Northern Quebec*. Quebec: Department of Justice.

Brock, Kathy. 1990. Aboriginal self-government: Canada by comparison. Commission on Folk Law and Legal Pluralism, Theme 1. Ottawa: Proceedings of the VI International Symposium.

Brodeur, Jean-Paul, and Yves Leguerrier. 1991. Policing and alternative dispute resolution. In: *Justice for the Cree*, ed. Jean-Paul Brodeur, Carol LaPrairie, and Roger McDonnell. James Bay, Quebec: Grand Council of the Crees.

Brodeur, Jean-Paul, Carol LaPrairie, and Roger McDonnell, eds. 1991. *Justice for the Cree; Final Report*. James Bay, Quebec: Grand Council of the Crees.

Bucknell, Brian. 1967. John Howard Sissons and the development of law in northern Canada. *Osgoode Hall Law Journal* 5.

Carswell, Margaret. 1984. Social controls among native peoples of the Northwest Territories in the pre-contact period. *Alberta Law Review* 22.

Case, David. 1984. *Alaska Natives and American Laws*. Fairbanks: University of Alaska Press.

Chapeskie, Andrew. 1990. Indigenous law, state law, renewable resources and formal indigenous self-government in northern regions. Commission on Folk Law and Legal Pluralism, Theme 1. Ottawa: Proceedings of the VI International Symposium.

Clark, Scott. 1992. Crime and community: Issues and directions in aboriginal justice. *Canadian Journal of Criminology* 34(3/4).

Cloke, Kenneth. 1971. The economic basis of law and state. In: *Law Against the People: Essays to Demystify Law, Order and the Courts*, ed. R. Lecourt. New York: Vintage.

Cohen, Stanley. 1982. Western crime control models in the developing world: Benign or malignant? In: *Research in Law, Deviance and Social Control*, ed. Steven Spitzer. Greenwich: JAI Press.

Conklin, William, and Gerard Ferguson. 1974. The Burnshine affair: Whatever happened to Drybones and equality before the law? *Chitty's Law Journal* 22(9).

Conn, Stephen. 1974. Bush Justice: *Sentencing Reforms – A Role for Council?* Fairbanks: Institute of Social, Economic and Government Research.

Conn, Stephen, and Arthur Hippler. 1974. Conciliation and arbitration in the native village and the urban ghetto. *Judicature* 58(5).

Copus, Gary, and Caralyn Holmes. 1990. North Slope police reports: A first look. *Alaska Justice Forum* 6(4).

Coulter, Robert. 1978. Indian conflicts and nonjudicial dispute settlement. *American Arbitration Association Journal* 33(4).

Coyle, Michael. 1986. Traditional Indian justice in Ontario: A role for the present. *Osgoode Hall Law Journal* 24(3).

Crawford, Anne. 1985. Outside the law and traditional communities in the Northwest Territories. Paper presented to the Western Regional Science Association, San Diego, California.

Cunneen, Chris. 1992. *Aboriginal Perspectives on Criminal Justice*. The Institute of Criminology Monograph Series, No. 1.

Daunton-Fear, Mary, and Arie Freiberg. 1977. Gum-tree justice: Aborigines and the courts. In: *The Australian Criminal Justice System*, ed. Duncan Chappell and Paul Wilson. Sydney: Henworth.

Dene Nation Crime Prevention Project Report. 1989. Yellowknife.

Depew, Robert. 1986. *Native Policing in Canada: A Review of Current Issues*. Ottawa: Ministry of the Solicitor General of Canada.

Depew, Robert. 1992. Policing native communities: Some principles and issues in organizational theory. *Canadian Journal of Criminology* 34(3/4).

DeWeerdt, Mark. 1984. The law through our eyes. In: *People of Light and Dark*, ed. Maja van Steensel. Ottawa: Department of Indian Affairs and Northern Development.

Dickson-Gilmore, E. Jane. 1990. Resurrecting the peace: Traditionalist approaches to separate justice in the Kahnawake Mohawk Nation. Commission on Folk Law and Legal Pluralism, Theme 1. Ottawa: Proceedings of the VI International Symposium.

Dickson-Gilmore, E. Jane. 1992. Finding the ways of the ancestors: Cultural change and the invention of tradition in the development of separate legal systems. *Canadian Journal of Criminology* 34(3/4).

Directorate of NWT Justice. n.d. *Community Justice Initiatives in the NWT*. Yellowknife, Northwest Territories.

Dumont, James. 1992. Aboriginal people and justice. Paper submitted to the National Round Table on Justice Issues of the Royal Commission on Aboriginal Peoples, Vol. 1, Tabs 2–4, Ottawa, Ontario.

Elberg, Nathan. 1983. Comprehensive claims, culture and customary law: The case of the Labrador Inuit. In: *Proceedings of the Commission on Folk Law and Legal Pluralism*, Volume 1, ed. Fons Strijbosch. Nijmegen, The Netherlands: Faculty of Law, Catholic University.

Fetzer, Philip. 1983. Jurisdictional decisions in Indian law: The importance of extralegal factors in judicial decision-making. *American Indian Law Review* 4(2).

Finkler, Harold. 1981. *Corrections in the Northwest Territories 1967-1981, with a Focus on the Incarceration of Inuit Offenders*. Ottawa: Department of Indian Affairs and Northern Development.

Finkler, Harold. 1983. Legal anthropology in the formulation of correctional policy in the Northwest Territories. Paper presented to the Commission on Folk Law and Legal Pluralism, Vancouver, B.C.

Finkler, Harold. 1992. Community participation in socio-legal control: The northern context. *Canadian Journal of Criminology* 34(3/4).

Francis, Robert. 1973. Justice northern style. Paper presented to the Muskox Circle.

French, Laurence, and Jim Hornbuckle. 1982. 1977-78: An analysis of Indian violence – the Cherokee example. *American Indian Quarterly* 3(4).

Fumoleau, Rene. 1975. *As Long as this Land Shall Last*. Toronto: McLelland & Stewart.

Gall, Gerald. 1983. *The Canadian Legal System*. Toronto: Carswell.

Geertz, Clifford. 1983. *Local Knowledge*. New York: Basic Books.

Giokas, John. 1992. How can the Canadian justice system be adapted to accommodate the concerns of aboriginal peoples? Paper presented to the National Round Table on Aboriginal Justice of the Royal Commission on Aboriginal Peoples, Ottawa, Ontario.

Gormley, Daniel. 1984. Aboriginal rights as natural rights. *Canadian Journal of Native Studies* 4(1).

Government of Alberta. 1991. *Report of the Task Force on the Criminal Justice System and its Impact on the Indian and Metis People of Alberta: Justice on Trial*. Edmonton, Alberta.

Government of Canada/Saskatchewan and the Federation of Saskatchewan Indian Nations. 1985. *Reflecting Indian Concerns and Values in the Justice System*. Regina, Saskatchewan.

Government of Manitoba. 1991. *Report of the Aboriginal Justice Inquiry of Manitoba*, Vols. 1 and 2. Winnipeg: Government of Manitoba.

Government of the Northwest Territories. Department of Justice. 1991. *Aboriginal Justice in the Northwest Territories*. Yellowknife, Northwest Territories.

Government of the Northwest Territories. Department of Social Services. 1990. *Myths Surround Spousal Assault*. Yellowknife: Spousal Assault Network, Government of the Northwest Territories.

Grant, Peter. 1982. The role of traditional law in contemporary cases. *Canadian Legal Aid Bulletin* 5(2/3).

Grant, Peter. 1990. Delgamuukw and others versus the Queen: The Gitksan-Wet'suwet'en land claims case in BC – pushing the boundaries of the recognition of the content of aboriginal jurisdiction. Commission on Folk Law and Legal Fluralism, Theme 1. Ottawa: Proceedings of the VI International Symposium.

Green, L.C. 1974. Tribal rights and equal rights. *Chitty's Law Journal* 22(3).

Griffiths, Curt. 1985. Addressing juvenile delinquency: The need for traditional and community-based structures of social control. In: *Proceedings of the Commission on Folk and Legal Pluralism*, ed. Harald Finkler. Ottawa: Department of Indian Affairs and Northern Development.

Griffiths, Curt, ed. 1990. *Preventing and Responding to Northern Crime*. Burnaby, B.C.: Northern Justice Society and Simon Fraser University.

Griffiths, Curt, and Allan Patenaude. 1988. Application of the criminal law to native Indians and Inuit in the Northwest Territories. Paper available from the Northern Justice Centre, Burnaby, B.C.

Griffiths, Curt, and Allan Patenaude. 1988. The use of community service orders and restitution in the Canadian North: The prospects and problems of localized corrections. Paper presented to the International Symposium on Restitution and Community Service Sentencing, Minneapolis.

Griffiths, Curt, and Colin Yerbury. 1983. Conflict and compromise: Canadian indigenous peoples and the law. Paper presented at the Commission on Folk Law and Legal Pluralism, Vancouver, B.C.

Griffiths, Curt, and Colin Yerbury. 1984. Natives and criminal justice policy: The case of native policing. *Canadian Journal of Criminology* 26(2).

Griffiths, Curt, Colin Yerbury, and Linda Weaver. 1983. Victimization of Canada's natives: The consequences of sociocultural deprivation. Paper presented at the XXXIII International Congress of Criminology, Vancouver, B.C.

Griffiths, Curt, Colin Yerbury, and Linda Weaver. 1987. Canadian natives: Victims of sociostructural deprivation? *Human Organization* 46(3).

Grossman, Toby, and Charlotte Goodluck. 1985. Understanding Indian sexual abuse and some issues defined in the tribal context. *American Indian Law Review Newsletter* 18(4).

Groves, Robert. 1990. Territoriality and aboriginal self-determination: Options for legal pluralism in Canada. Commission on Folk Law and Legal Pluralism, Theme 1. Ottawa: Proceedings of the VI International Symposium.

Halliday, W.E. 1937. *Canada Mines and Resources Bulletin* 89.

Harding, James. 1990. Strategies to reduce the over-incarceration of aboriginal people in Canada: A research consultation. Aboriginal Justice Series Report No. 1. Regina: Prairie Justice Research Institute, University of Regina.

Harding, James, and Beryl Forgay. 1991. *Breaking Down the Walls: A Bibliography on the Pursuit of Aboriginal Justice*. Regina: Prairie Justice Research Institute, University of Regina.

Harding, James, and Bruce Spence. 1991. *Annotated Bibliography of Aboriginal-controlled Justice Programs in Canada*. Regina: Prairie Justice Research Institute, University of Regina.

Harring, Sidney. 1982. Native American crime in the United States. In: *Indians and Criminal Justice*, ed. Lawrence French. Totowa: Allenheld-Osmun.

Havermann, Paul. 1982. The Regina native counsel project: A civilian perspective on the delivery of legal services to people of Indian ancestry in the city. Canadian *Legal Aid Bulletin* 5(1).

Havermann, Paul. 1983. The indigenization of social control in Canada. Paper presented to the XI International Congress of Anthropological and Ethnological Sciences.

Havermann, Paul. 1989. Law, state and Canada's indigenous people: Pacification by coercion and consent. In: *Law and Society: A Critical Perspective*, ed. T. Caputo, M. Kennedy, C. Reasons, and A. Brannigan. Toronto: Harcourt Brace.

Haysom, Veryan, and Jeff Richstone. 1987. Customizing law in the Territories: Proposal for a task force on customary law in Nunavut. *Inuit Studies* 11(1).

Hazelhurst, Kayleen. 1983. Justice programs for aboriginal and other indigenous communities: Australia, New Zealand, Canada, Fiji, Papua-New Guinea. Proceedings No. 7, Australian Institute of Criminology, Sydney, Australia.

Helliwell, John. 1977. The distribution of economic benefits from a pipeline. In: *Dene Nation: The Colony Within*, ed. Mel Watkins. Toronto: University of Toronto Press.

Helm, June. 1968. The nature of Dogrib socioterritorial bands. In: *Man the Hunter*, ed. R. Lee and I. DeVore. Chicago: Aldine.

Helm, June. 1973. *Subarctic Athapaskan Bibliography*. Iowa City: Iowa University Press.

Helm, June, and Beryl Gillespie. 1981. Dogrib oral tradition as history: War and peace in the 1820's. *Journal of Anthropological Research* 37(1).

Helm, June, and Eleanor Leacock. 1971. The hunting tribes of the Subarctic. In: *North American Indians in Historical Perspective*, ed. E. Leacock and N. Larrie. New York: Random House.

Hemmington, Rick. 1988. Jurisdiction of future tribal courts in Canada: Learning from the American experience. *Canadian Native Law Review* 2.

Hippler, Arthur, and Stephen Conn. 1972. *Traditional Athapascan Law Ways and their Relationship to Contemporary Problems of Bush Justice: Some Preliminary Observations on Structure and Function*. Fairbanks: Institute of Social, Economic and Government Research.

Hippler, Arthur, and Stephen Conn. 1974. The changing legal culture of the north Alaska Eskimo. *Ethnos* 2(2).

Hobsbawn, Eric. 1983. Inventing traditions. In: *The Invention of Traditions*, ed. E. Hobsbawn and Terence Ranger.Cambridge: Cambridge University Press.

Huggins, Martha. 1985. Approaches to crime and societal development. In: *Comparative Social Research*, Vol. 8, ed. Richard Tomasson. Greenwich: JAI Press.

Hulkrantz, Ake. 1973. The Hare Indians: Notes on traditional culture and religion, past and present. *Ethnos* 38(1).

Hunt, Constance. 1976. Creative law in the North. *Canadian Welfare* 52(7).

Hunt, Constance. 1986. The law and its institutions in the North. Paper presented to the Canadian Institute of Resource Law, University of Calgary, Calgary, Alberta.

Hylton, John. 1981. Locking up Indians in Saskatchewan. *Canadian Ethnic Studies* 13(3).

Hylton, John. 1982. The native offender in Saskatchewan: Some implications for crime prevention programming. *Canadian Journal of Criminology* 24.

Jackson, Michael. 1984. The articulation of native rights in Canadian law. *UBC Law Review* 18(2).

Jackson, Michael. 1989. Locking up natives in Canada. *UBC Law Review* 23.

Jefferson, Christie. 1980. White justice: Should native people respect Canadian law? *Tawow* 8(1).

Johnson, Martha, and Robert Ruttan. 1993. *Traditional Dene Environmental Knowledge*. Dene Cultural Institute, Hay River, Northwest Territories.

Kane, Doug. 1984. Customary law: A preliminary assessment of the arguments for recognition and an identification of the possible ways of defining the term. A working paper for the Canada-Saskatchewan/ FSIN Project, Saskatoon, Saskatchewan.

Kelley, Jane. 1977. Observations on crisis cult activities in the MacKenzie Basin. Paper presented at the Ninth Annual Conference of the Archaeological Association, Calgary, Alberta.

Keon-Cohen, Bryan. 1981. Native justice in Australia, Canada and the United States: A comparative analysis. *Monash University Law Review* 7.

Keon-Cohen, Bryan. 1984. *Aborigines and the Law*. Sydney: Allen and Unwin.

Kidder, Robert. 1979. Toward an integrated theory of imposed law. In: *The Imposition of Law*, ed. S. Burman and B.E. Harrel-Bond. New York: Academic Press.

Kimbell, R.E. 1990. In the matter of judicial discretion and the imposition of default orders. *The Criminal Law Quarterly* 32.

Kimmerly, Roger. 1980. A circuit judge looks at old crow. *Liaison* 6(11).

Kimmerly, Roger. 1981. Sentencing in old crow. *Canadian Legal Aid Bulletin*.

Krosenbrink-Gelissen, Lillian E. 1990. Sexual equality as an aboriginal right: Canada's aboriginal women in the constitutional process on aboriginal matters, 1982-87. Commission on Folk Law and Legal Pluralism, Theme 1. Ottawa: Proceedings of the VI International Symposium.

La Rusic, Ignatius. 1990. Aspects of local control in state social security: Incorporating traditional values in the income security program for Cree hunters and trappers. Commission on Folk Law and Legal Pluralism, Theme 1. Ottawa: Proceedings of the VI International Symposium.

Lambert, Carmen. 1991. What if the Mohawks were right? Paper presented at the Canadian Anthropology Society Conference, Harry Hawthorne Lecture, University of Western Ontario, London, Ontario.

LaPrairie, Carol. 1992. Aboriginal crime and justice: Explaining the present, exploring the future. *Canadian Journal of Criminology* 34(3/4).

LaPrairie, Carol, and Eddie Diamond. 1992. Who owns the problem? Crime and disorder in James Bay Cree communities. *Canadian Journal of Criminology* 34(3/4).

LaPrairie, Carol, and Yves Leguerrier. 1991. *Communities, Crimes and Order. Justice for the Cree.* James Bay, Quebec: Grand Council of the Crees.

Leacock, Eleanor. 1980. *Women and Colonization: Anthropological Perspectives.* New York: Praeger.

Lee, Nella. 1988. Rural crime rates high. *Alaska Justice Forum* 5(2).

Legat, Allice. 1991. *Report of the Traditional Knowledge Working Group.* Yellowknife: Government of the Northwest Territories, Department of Culture and Communications.

Levy, Jerrold, and Stephen Kunitz. 1971. Indian reservations, anomie and social pathologies. *Southwestern Journal of Anthropology* 27(2).

Lillies, Chief Justice Heino. 1989. Some problems in the administration of justice in remote and isolated communities. Paper presented at the CIAJ Conference, Kananaskis, Alberta.

Lowe, Mick. 1985. Wrist watch justice. *Canadian Lawyer,* June.

MacDonald, Roderick. 1992. Recognizing and legitimating aboriginal justice: Implications for a reconstruction of non-aboriginal legal systems in Canada. Paper presented to the National Round Table on Aboriginal Justice of the Royal Commission on Aboriginal Peoples, Ottawa, Ontario.

MacInnis, Todd. 1990. Native salmon fishing at Kingsclear, NB: An anthropological study of law and dispute. Commission on Folk Law and Legal Pluralism, Theme 1. Ottawa: Proceedings of the VI International Symposium.

Macklem, Patrick. 1992. Aboriginal justice, the distribution of legislative authority and the judicative provisions of the Constitution Act of 1867. Paper presented to the National Round Table on Aboriginal Justice of the Royal Commission on Aboriginal Peoples, Ottawa, Ontario.

Maddock, Kenneth. 1989. Aboriginal customary law. In: *Aboriginal Peoples and the Law,* ed. Bradford Morse. Ottawa: Carleton University Press.

Mahoney, Kathleen, ed. 1992. *Report on the Geneva Workshop on Judicial Treatment of Domestic Violence.* Geneva: International Project to Promote Fairness in Judicial Processes.

Mandamin, Tony. 1992. Aboriginal justice systems: Relationships. Paper presented to the National Round Table on Aboriginal Justice of the Royal Commission on Aboriginal Peoples, Ottawa, Ontario.

McDonnell, Roger. 1983. Symbolic orientation and systematic turmoil: Centring on the Kaska notion of Dene. *Canadian Journal of Anthropology* 4(1).

McDonnell, Roger. 1992a. Contextualizing the investigation of customary law in contemporary native communities. *Canadian Journal of Criminology* 34(3/4).

McDonnell, Roger. 1992b. *Justice for the Cree: Customary beliefs and practices.* Report for the Grand Council of the Crees [Quebec], Cree regional authority. James Bay, Quebec: Grand Council of the Crees.

McNeish, June Helm. 1958. The Lynx Point people: A northern Athabascan band. Ph.D. dissertation, Department of Anthropology, University of Chicago.

Moeller, Kim. 1979. *Alcohol Abuse and the Police in Rural Alaska.* Barrow: North Slope Borough Department of Public Safety.

Monture-Okanee, Patricia. 1992. Reclaiming justice: Aboriginal women and justice initiatives in the 1990's. Paper presented to the National Round Table on Aboriginal Justice of the Royal Commission on Aboriginal Peoples, Ottawa, Ontario.

Moore, Sally Falk. 1978. *Law as Process: An Anthropological Approach.* London: Routledge and Kegan Paul.

Morrow, Phyllis, and Mary C. Pete. 1990. Cultural adoption on trial: Cases from southwestern Alaska. Commission on Folk Law and Legal Pluralism, Theme 1. Ottawa: Proceedings of the VI International Symposium.

Morrow, W.C. 1981. Adapting our justice system to the cultural needs of Canada's North. In: *Crime and Criminal Justice in Europe and Canada*, ed. L. Knafla. Waterloo: Wilfrid Laurier University Press.

Morse, Bradford. 1980a. Indian and Inuit family law and the Canadian legal system. *American Law Review VII.*

Morse, Bradford. 1980b. *Indian Tribal Courts in the United States: A Model for Canada?* Saskatoon: Native Law Centre, University of Saskatoon.

Morse, Bradford. 1983. Indigenous law and state legal systems: Conflict and compatibility. Paper presented at the Commission on Contemporary Folk Law and Legal Pluralism, Vancouver, B.C.

Morse, Bradford. 1989. *Aboriginal People and the Law: Indian, Metis and Inuit Rights in Canada.* Ottawa: Carleton University Press.

Morse, Bradford, and Linda Lock. 1988. *Native Offenders: Perceptions of the Criminal Justice System.* Ottawa: Department of Justice.

Nahanee, Teresa. 1992. Dancing with a gorilla: Aboriginal women, justice and the Charter. Paper presented to the National Round Table on Aboriginal Justice of the Royal Commission on Aboriginal Peoples, Ottawa, Ontario.

Napoleon, Harold. 1990. Yu'ya'Raq: The Way of the human being. Paper presented to the Conference on Northern Justice, Sitka, Alaska.

Northern Justice Collection Bibliography. 1991. Whitehorse: Yukon College Resource Centre.

Patenaude, Allan. 1989. Whose law? Whose justice? Two conflicting systems of law and justice in Canada's Northwest Territories. Essay available from the Northern Justice Centre, Simon Fraser University, Burnaby, B.C.

Patenaude, Allan, and Curt Griffiths. 1989. Dependency and deviance among Inuit in the Canadian Arctic. Paper presented to the School of Criminology, Simon Fraser University, Burnaby, B.C.

Patenaude, Allan, Darryl Woods, and Curt Griffiths. 1992. Indigenous peoples in the Canadian correctional system: Critical issues and the prospects for localized corrections. *Journal of Contemporary Criminal Justice.*

Pellat, Anna. 1991. An international review of child welfare policy and practice in relation to aboriginal people. Report to the Canadian Research Institute for Law and the Family, University of Calgary, Calgary, Alberta.

Perry, Richard. 1989. Matrilineal descent in a hunting context: The Athapaskan case. *Ethnology* 28(1).

Pete, Jacob, and Darlene Robins. 1989. *Dene Nation Crime Prevention Project. Final Report.* Dene Nation, Yellowknife, Northwest Territories.

Peterson, Catherine. 1992. *The Justice House. Report of the Special Advisor on Gender Equality.* Yellowknife: Department of Justice.

Petitot, Emil. 1891. *Autour du grand las des esclaves.* Paris: Nouvelle Librairie Parisienne.

Piddock, Stuart. 1985. Land, community, corporation: Intercultural correlation between ideas of land in Dene and Inuit tradition and in Canadian law. Ph.D. dissertation, Department of Anthropology, University of British Colombia, Vancouver, B.C.

Ponting, J. Rick, and Roger Gibbins. 1980. *Out of Irrelevance: A Socio-political Introduction to Indian Affairs in Canada.* Toronto: Butterworths.

Poposil, Leopold. 1971. *The Anthropology of Law: A Comparative Theory.* San Francisco: Cummings.

Poposil, Leopold. 1978. *The Ethnography of Law: A Comparative Theory.* San Francisco: Cummings.

Poposil, Leopold. 1979. Legally induced culture change in New Guinea. In: *The Imposition of Law,* ed. S. Burman and B.E. Harrell-Bond. San Francisco: Cummings.

Rasing, Wim. 1984. On conflict management with Nomadic Inuit: An ethnological essay. Ph.D. dissertation, Department of Cultural Anthropology, Catholic University of Nijmegen, The Netherlands.

Reasons, Charles. 1977. Native offenders and correctional policy. *Crime et/and Justice* 4.

Richstone, Jeff. 1983. The Inuit and customary law: Constitutional papers. In: *Proceedings of the Commission on Folk Law and Legal Pluralism,* ed. Fons Strijbosch. Nijmegen, The Netherlands: Faculty of Law, Catholic University.

Ridington, Robin. 1988.*The Prophet Dance among the Dunne-za.* Vancouver: University of British Columbia Press.

Ridington, Robin. 1988. Knowledge, power and the individual in Subarctic hunting societies. *American Anthropologist* 90.

Ridington, Robin. 1989. *Trails to Heaven*. Lincoln: University of Nebraska Press.

Riffenburg, Arthur. 1964. Cultural influences and crime among Indian Americans of the Southwest. *Federal Probation* 23 (1).

Ross, Rupert. 1992. *Dancing with a Ghost: Exploring Indian Reality*. Markham: Octopus.

Rouland, Norbert. 1979. Les modes juridiques des conflits chez les Inuits. *Etudes Inuit* 3, Université Laval, Québec.

Royal Commission on Aboriginal Peoples Research Committee. 1992. *Aboriginal Justice Inquiries and Commissions: An Update*. Ottawa, Ontario.

Ryan, Joan, and Michael Robinson. 1990. Implementing participatory action research in the Canadian North: A case study of the Gwich'in language and cultural project. *Culture* 10(2).

Ryan, Joan, and Michael Robinson. 1992. Participatory action research: An examination of two northern case studies. Paper prepared for the Arctic Institute, Dene Cultural Institute and the Royal Commission on Aboriginal Peoples. Available at the Arctic Institute of North America, University of Calgary, Calgary, Alberta.

Saddle Lake Indian Band. 1986. Indian jurisprudence and mediation the Indian way: A case review of the Saddle Lake tribal justice system. Paper presented to the Conference on Mediation, Winnipeg, Manitoba.

Samson, Alana, L. Douglass, K. Stocker, S. Casavant, and E. Baker. 1991. *Childhood Sexual Abuse: A Booklet for First Nations Adult Survivors*. Victoria Women's Sexual Assault Centre, Victoria, B.C.

Sanders, Douglas. 1977. Lawyers and Indians in the Canadian North. Paper presented to the Faculty of Law, University of British Columbia, Vancouver, B.C.

Savishinsky, Joel S. 1974. *The Trail of the Hare: Environment and Stress in a Sub-Arctic Community*. New York: Gordon and Breach.

Schecter, Elaine. 1983. The Greenland criminal code and the limits to legal pluralism. Paper presented to the XI International Congress of Anthropological and Ethnological Sciences, Vancouver, B.C.

Schecter, Elaine. 1985. Institutionalizing criminality in Greenland. In: *Indigenous Law and the State*, ed. Bradford Morse and Gordon Woodman. Providence, RI: Foris.

Schuh, Cornelia. n.d. Justice on the northern frontier: Early murder trials of native accused. Paper presented to Faculty of Law, University of Toronto.

Schwartz, Bryan. 1990. A separate aboriginal justice system? *Manitoba Law Journal* 19(1).

Shelley, Louise. 1981. *Crime and Modernization*. Carbondale: Southern Illinois University Press.

Stetson, Catherine Baker. 1981. Decriminalizing tribal codes: A response to Oliphant. *American Indian Law Review* 9.

Stillwagen, E. 1981. Anti-Indian agitation and economic interests. *Monthly Review* 33(6).

Strickland, Rennard. 1973. American Indian law and the spirit world. *American Indian Law Review* 1/2.

Svensson, Tom. 1990. The attainment of limited self-determination among the Sami in recent years. Commission on Folk Law and Legal Pluralism, Theme 1. Ottawa: Proceedings of the VI International Symposium.

Tallis, C.F. 1980. Sentencing in the North. In: *New Directions in Sentencing*, ed. Brian Grosman. Toronto: Butterworths.

Tanner, Adrian. 1979. *Bringing Home Animals: Religious Ideology and Mode of Production of the Mistassini Cree Hunters*. Social and Economic Studies, No. 23. Memorial University, St. Johns, Newfoundland.

Testart, Alain. 1988. Some major problems in the social anthropology of hunter-gatherers. *Current Anthropology* 29(1).

Thorne, Brian. 1990. An introduction to aboriginal justice and the function of an elders council. Paper written for the First Nations South Island Tribal Council, Victoria, B.C.

Thorpe, Dagmar. 1993. In the year of indigenous people 1993: The founding concept paper. Paper presented to Ma Ta Sa Ma E Winana, A Resource for Traditional Indigenous People, Yale University, New Haven, Connecticut.

Tooker, E., ed. 1979. *The Development of Political Organization in Native North America*. Proceedings of the American Ethnological Society, Washington, D.C.

Turpel, Mary Ellen. 1990. Indigenous self-determination and legal pluralism. Commission on Folk Law and Legal Pluralism, Theme 1. Ottawa: Proceedings of the VI International Symposium.

Turpel, Mary Ellen. 1992. On the question of adapting the Canadian criminal justice system for aboriginal peoples: Don't fence me in. Paper presented to the National Round Table on Aboriginal Justice of the Royal Commission on Aboriginal Peoples, Ottawa, Ontario.

Tyler, Kenneth. 1985. The recognition of aboriginal customary law by the Canadian courts. Working paper prepared for the Joint Canada-Saskatchewan/FSIN Project on Aboriginal Customary Law, Saskatoon, Saskatchewan.

Van Dyke, E.W., and K.C. Jamont. 1980. Through Indian Eyes: *Perspectives of Indian Special Constables on the Third Program in "F" Division*. RCMP Report, Regina, Saskatchewan.

Vanstone, James. 1974. The subsistence base and settlement patterns. In: *Athapaskan Adaptations: Hunters and Fishermen of the Subarctic Forests*, ed. James Vanstone. Chicago: Aldine.

Verdun-Jones, Simon. 1978. Natives in the Canadian criminal justice system: An overview. Paper presented to the American Society of Criminology, Dallas, Texas.

Webber, Jeremy. 1992. Individuality, equality and difference: Justifications for a parallel system of aboriginal justice. Paper presented to the National Round Table on Aboriginal Justice of the Royal Commission on Aboriginal Peoples, Ottawa, Ontario.

Weerdt, Mark K. 1974. The law through our eyes. In: *People of Light and Dark,* ed. Maja van Steensel. Ottawa: Department of Indian Affairs and Northern Development.

Yabsley, Gary. 1984. *Nunavut and Inuit Customary Law.* Report to the Nunavut Constitutional Forum, Ottawa, Ontario.

Zion, James. 1983. The Navaho Peacemaker Court: Deference to the old and accommodation to the new. Paper presented to the Commission on Folk Law and Legal Pluralism, Ottawa, Ontario.

Zion, James. 1984. Peacemaking in Saskatchewan. Paper prepared for the Joint Canada-Saskatchewan FSIN Studies of the Justice System in Saskatchewan, Regina, Saskatchewan.

Zion, James. 1992. Taking Justice Back: American Indian Perspectives. Solicitor, Courts of the Navajo Nation.

Zlotkin, N.K. 1983. Judicial recognition of aboriginal customary law in Canada: Selected marriage and adoption cases. In: *Symposia on Folk Law and Legal Pluralism,* ed. Harald Finkler. XIth International Congress of Anthropological and Ethnological Sciences, Vancouver, B.C.

Index

adaptations of non-Dene system: 66
adoption: 48
adulthood: 47
alcohol:
    abuse of, xxix, 9, 104
    CAC policies, 9
    prevention, 104
    sobriety, support for, xxix, 10
Arctic Institute of North America: iii,
        viii, xii, xiv
    project assistance, ixxv
author:
    biases, x
    voice, x

bad medicine, 55
balances (animals, spirits/humans):
        2–4, 23, 26
breaches of Dogrib rules: xxvii, 26,
        33–34, 57–58, 90–91
bush camps, traditional: 1, 23, 25

changes/transitions: 109–110, 118–
        119

children:
    birth 42, 43
    expectations of, 45
    pubescence, 46
    raising, 43–45
Community Advisory Committee:
        viii, xxv, xxvi, xxxi
    court observations: 20
    membership, xi, xxvi, xxxi
    policies, 9
    selection of, 6
    tasks, xi
community councils:
    Band, iii, xiii
    Hamlet, xii, xiii
    partnership with, xiii, xxv
Community Education Committee:
        viii
    marten case, 87–88
    teaching Dogrib language and
        skills, 68
conferences attended: 21–22

conflicts, between Dene and non-
    Dene
  belief systems, 3
  Charter of Rights, 92
  customs, rules and laws, 90–95,
    101
  justice concepts, 66, 89, 101
  justice systems 95–98
consensus:
  achieving, 106
  concepts, xxviii, 4, 90
  regional, xxxi
courts:
  affidavits, 19
  community justice committee, 19–
    20
  community perceptions of, 19
  concept of Dene Justice Project, 19
  contradictions, 21
  differences between, 18
  future joint ventures, 100
  interpreters, 18
  justice of the peace, 18
  observations of, 18, 20–21
  officers, 18, 98
  Supreme, 19
  Territorial, 18–19
court cases:
  custody, Apple-Bishop, 80–87
  theft, Marie Adele Moosenose, 19,
    73–80
  theft, marten pelts, 87–88

Dene Cultural Institute: iii, viii, xii,
    xiv, xxv
  decisions, 4
  tasks, xiii, 21
Dene language: 2, 13
Dene Meni Coop: xii
Denendeh:
  First Nations, 1, 40
  region, 1, 2, 40
Dogrib:
  contact period, 2–3, 58–62
  Divisional Board of Education,
    xiii, xiv, xxv
  fur trade, 3

reclaiming social control, xxviii,
    xxix, 70–72
  society, 2
  treaty 11, 59–60

elders:
  and children, 42
  educational use of, 105–106
  good words, 40
  harsh words, 40–41
  interviewees, xxxii
  making/changing rules, xxvi

family rules: xxvi, 37–38
  extended, 37
  life cycle, 38–39
  living arrangements, 40
  marriage arrangements/
    preferences, 38–40
  separation, 41, 48
  spousal violence, 41
fishing: 26, 31–33,

gathering, 26, 33
government (Canada):
  Employment and Immigration,
    xiv, xxv
  Justice (Aboriginal Directorate),
    xiv, xxv
  Social Sciences and Humanities
    Research Council, viii, xiii,
    xxv, 5
government (Northwest Territories):
  Culture and Communications, xiii,
    xiv, xxv
  Justice, ix, xiii, xiv, xxv
  Justice of the Peace, viii

healing:
  needs, 104
  process, xxx
Hudson's Bay Company: viii, 37
  fur traders, 59–60
hunting: 28–31
  natural resource rules, xxvi, 23, 26
  enforcement of rules, xxvii
  partnerships, 26
  rituals, 27–28

interviews:
    development of guidelines, 15–18
    elders interviewed, xxxii
    topics, 26–27, 38, 51–52

judgments:
    traditional circle, xviii, xxx, 39
justice committees:
    confusion about, 19–20
    Dogrib proposal, 106

Lac La Martre Dene Justice Project:
    Dogrib/English literacy, 13
    early consultation process, 4–5
    funding search, xiv, xv, xxv, 4–5
    interview guidelines, 15–18
    reporting, 11
    selection process, Dogrib
        researchers, xv, 6–7
    training process, 5, 11, 13–15
language:
    Dogrib literacy, 68
leadership:
    chiefs: kw'ati [elected], xi, xii, 38,
        59
    responsibilities of, xxxvi, 53–55
    special helpers, 55–56; diviners,
        56; gifted persons, 31, 33, 38,
        55, 63; jesters, 56; prophets, 56
    traditional chiefs: k'aowo, xxvii, 34,
        42, 53, 55, 59, 63; yabahti, xxvi,
        xxvii, 38, 42, 53, 55, 59, 63
    women, 55
literature: reflections on
    Dene–non-Dene counterpoints,
        119–125
    ethnographic issues, 111–119
    philosophical, moral, political
        issues, 125–132

map, NWT Dogrib area, xiv
marten, theft of: 87–88
methodology: x, xxv, 51

natural resource rules, xxvi, 23, 26
Northern Justice Society, xiv
Northwest Trading Company, 59

Participatory Action Research: viii, 5
    benefits associated with, 11
    community issues, 6–8
    consequences, unanticipated, 19
    feminist issues, 9
    pros and cons, 7–11
    methodology, x, xxvi, 51
pilot project to follow: 107–108
political rules:
    governance, xxvi, 51–52, 57–62
    social control enforcement, 26
    restitution, 91
    summary, 62–64
principal investigator: viii, xv, xxv
project director: viii, xv, xxv
pubescence: 46

recommendations: xxix, xxx, 103–108
research team: xxv, xxxi, 6–7
Roman Catholic: viii
    activities, 3, 39
    church, 37
    impact on Dene people, 3, 59–60,
        103
    priests' arrival, 3, 59
Royal Canadian Mounted Police: viii
    actions, xiii, 52
    arrival in area, 59–60
    constables in community, xii, xiii
    discretionary power, 96
    early posts, 37

seasonal round: 1
    activities, 25
    chart of, 24
stewardship: xxvi, 23, 27–28
summaries:
    family rules, 49–50
    natural resource rules, 34–35
    political rules, 62–64

Technical Advisory Committee: viii
    members, xxxi
    role, xii, xxvi
traditional justice concepts:
    absence of "not guilty, " xxviii, 4,
        90
    system, xxx

traditional knowledge: 65
    Dogrib, xiii, xxvi, 65
    Gwich'in, xiii, 22
    North Slavey, xiii, 22
traditional rules: xxvi
    breaches, xxvii, xxviii, 26, 33–34,
        57–58, 90–91
    division of labour, 26
    enforcement, xxvii, 26
    family, xxvi, 37–38
    fishing, 26, 31–33
    gathering, 26, 33
    governance, xxvi, 51–52, 57–62
    hunting, 28–31
    men/women, xxvii, 27
    natural resource, xxvi, 23, 26
    partnerships, 26
    pubescence, 46
    restitution/reconciliation, 91
    rituals, 26–27
    social control, 26

    stewardship, xxvi, 23, 27–28
    tests of, 103
    trapping, 26, 31
translation: ix
    difficulties with, ix
    interpreting skills, 13
    official languages, x
    translators, xii
trapping: 26, 31
treaty 11: 59–60

values: xxviii, xxix
    caring, 70
    respect, 66
    responsibility, 70
    self-discipline, 67
    self-reliance, 68
    sharing, 69
verification: x
    community, xxx, 11
    Dogrib region, xxx, 11

"Tigger," friend of many children and the PI's companion.

MIKE ROBINSON

Joan Ryan.